What Experts Are Saying About *Contract to Unite America*

"This book is for every American who is fed up with dysfunction and partisan paralysis in Washington and looking for how to fix it. Neal has the real-world experience running for office as an independent, with some amazing lessons learned. The ideas in *Contract to Unite America* ought to be required reading for congressional orientation."

—Glenn Nye, former member of Congress and CEO of the Center for the Study of the Presidency and Congress

"We are in a dark moment in American politics and the only way out is to fix the system itself. There are so many terrible rules and laws governing how we elect people and how Congress operates that make pragmatic problem-solving impossible. In this book, Neal offers a thoughtful and urgent prescription for how to repair our democracy before it's too late."

—Nancy Jacobson, founder and CEO of No Labels

"From ending gerrymandering to establishing ranked-choice voting, Neal Simon's *Contract to Unite America* represents an important next step in the debate over how to protect and strengthen American democracy. His proposals, which are the product of his unique experience as a political philanthropist, an independent candidate, and a leading reform advocate, should be studied by all Americans working to preserve our republic."

—Evan McMullin, executive director of Stand Up Republic and 2016 independent candidate for president

"Congress is broken, but it is not beyond repair. Neither is our country. Neal Simon recognizes that most dysfunctional politicians are good people responding to very bad incentives. This book offers practical solutions that would alter that equation—and produce a more collaborative and effective government."

—Jason Grumet, CEO of Bipartisan Policy Center

"If you are tired of establishment politics and of politicians choosing special interests over the public good, this book is for you. Neal Simon explains how political system failure is causing these problems, and provides a user manual for anyone looking for real, lasting solutions to America's growing political crisis."

—Josh Silver, CEO of RepresentUs

"Having once had the most centrist voting record in Congress, I know from experience how our current political system incentivizes division over consensus. Neal Simon offers common-sense solutions that would change Washington for the better. A must-read for anyone who wants to know the most effective and realistic antidotes to the epidemic of partisanship infecting American politics today. Written in a fast-paced and readable style, these prescriptions for reform are just what the doctor ordered."

—Jason Altmire, former member of Congress and author of *Dead Center: How Political Polarization Divided America and What We Can Do About It*

"Our government is failing to address our largest challenges—from healthcare costs and climate change to the soaring national debt. Simon lays out a sensible, workable, and nonpartisan agenda that could hold the key to putting us back on track. This is a book every member of Congress should read, not to mention every voter who wants to get our country working again."

—Maya MacGuineas, CEO of the Committee for a Responsible Federal Budget

"This wonderfully accessible and compelling book outlines not just what is wrong with our broken political system but how we can piece our democracy back together again. It's a manual for change that every American should read and unite behind."

—Nick Penniman, CEO of Issue One

"Americans always have rallied in times of crisis to keep our promise of equal citizens, human liberty, and effective self-government alive. To see how we will do so again now, read Neal Simon's *Contract to Unite America*—this is the call to action we've been waiting for."

—Jeff Clements, president of American Promise

"We have a governance crisis. We can wring our hands and blame our political opponents, which is how we got here, or we can roll up our sleeves and begin repairing the system. Neal Simon's book is packed with thoughtful, practical, and achievable ideas for doing the latter."

—Charles Wheelan, author of *The Centrist Manifesto* and founder of Unite America

CONTRACT TO
UNITE
AMERICA

RealClear
PUBLISHING

For more information, please contact:
Amplify Publishing, an imprint of Mascot Books
620 Herndon Parkway, Suite 320
Herndon, VA 20170
info@mascotbooks.com

Library of Congress Control Number: 2019916321

CPSIA Code: PRFRE1219A
ISBN: 978-1-64543-064-3

Printed in Canada

CONTRACT TO UNITE AMERICA

Ten Reforms to Reclaim Our Republic

Neal Simon

Table of Contents

Many young people are concerned about why we live in a world of constant—and utterly ineffective—partisan warfare. One 25-year-old once said to Neal, while he was on the campaign trail: "My generation does not understand why our government is a blue team fighting against a red team. Why isn't it one team working together for the common good of Americans?"

That 25-year-old is not alone. Many college students wonder why our elected leaders fail to take essential policy steps on education, immigration, healthcare, and job creation, and instead seem focused on winning the daily news cycle.

Neal invites you to expose your students to a set of political reforms that would change the polarizing incentives for American candidates and lawmakers. *Contract to Unite America* is based upon his 2018 U.S. Senate campaign, in which he ran as an independent, and includes extensive research of other races from around the country. Each reform is supported by 60 percent or more of Americans, and are practical solutions for improved government for all generations to come.

Neal appreciates your time and welcomes your feedback: **njbs@nealsimon.com.**

ContractToUnite.com

Author's Note

Mitch McConnell and Chuck Schumer, this book is not for you. Sorry, Nancy Pelosi and Kevin McCarthy, it's not for you either.

I mean no disrespect to America's current congressional leaders, Republican or Democrat. This is not personal. Likewise, if you are part of what the media calls the "base" of Republican Party or the Democratic Party and you harbor visceral hatred for the other side, you should probably stop reading now. If you think the most critical political objective is to defeat the other party, this isn't your playbook.

If you believe it is more important to get one more person from your party elected than to solve one more problem for America, I'm not your guy. If you think President Trump can do no wrong, you're not my target audience. The same is true if you cannot come up with one thing the Trump administration has gotten right. If you are among either the 8 percent of Americans identified in a well-known "hidden tribes" survey who are "progressive activists" or the 6 percent who are "devoted conservatives," I may not be able to reach you.

This book is intended to reach people like the twenty-five-year-old Maryland accountant who told me last year while I was campaigning for a seat in the United States Senate, "My generation does not understand why our government is a 'blue' team fighting against a 'red' team."

"Why," he added, "isn't it one team working together for the common good of Americans?"

He gave voice to a frustration shared by millions of Americans. It's one of the reasons I ran for office in 2018, and addressing that concern is why I wrote this book.

Contract to Unite America is also for those who yearn for the days when President Ronald Reagan could work effectively with House Speaker Thomas P. "Tip" O'Neill Jr. to fix Social Security's looming insolvency. Yes, Republicans and Democrats once knew how to negotiate with each other—and how to compromise.

This book is for the record number of Americans who think government is currently the problem rather than the solution. It is for the 46 percent of us who identify as neither Republicans nor Democrats—and for members of the two parties who realize that neither side has a monopoly on wisdom or good intentions.

This book is for the 85,964 people who voted for me in my run for U.S. Senate.

Finally, this book is for family, starting with my amazing wife, Jennifer, who is a lifelong Democrat who sometimes votes, and even argues, against her own party. It is for my three children, each of whom has chosen to register as an independent and who have learned to challenge ideas presented by any politician or party. And it is for their children and their children's children, to whom I hope we will leave a stronger, more unified nation.

Introduction

Election Day came two weeks early for me in 2018.

On October 23, at 10:45 p.m., I was sitting on the couch in our family room where, after channel surfing for a few minutes, I settled on *Pretty Woman*, a movie I'd seen many times. At that moment, I was running for the U.S. Senate and was nervously awaiting a text from Steve Crim, my campaign manager, about the new poll numbers that would reveal whether we still had a plausible path to victory.

I like *Pretty Woman*, partly because I'm a sucker for sappy love stories and also because my wife, Jennifer, has been told many times that she looks like the film's star, Julia Roberts. At this moment, Roberts and Richard Gere were keeping my mind off the pending survey results. Under any circumstances, unseating Maryland's Democratic incumbent Senator Ben Cardin would have been a long shot, since 55 percent of Maryland's registered voters[1] are Democrats and our state hasn't sent a non-Democrat to the Senate since 1980. But what I was trying to do was even harder. I was running as an independent, unaffiliated with either major party, and without the resources and brands that benefit their candidates.

Since launching the campaign in February, I had made multiple visits to all twenty-three Maryland counties and the city of Baltimore, spreading my message of uniting the country and changing the way Washington works. In mid-September, the first public opinion poll had me at 8 percent. After a televised debate in early October where I faced off with Senator Cardin and Republican challenger Tony Campbell, I was at 18 percent. It was an encouraging trajectory, suggesting that a path to victory, which Steve had laid out months earlier, was possible.

To stay on track, we needed to jump to around 28 percent. This would create what my friend Greg Orman calls "escape velocity." Greg, who had run as an independent for a U.S. Senate seat in Kansas and nearly won four years earlier, believes that once independents get into the mid-twenties in polls, they escape the "spoiler argument" used by both Democrats and Republicans. We were cautiously optimistic, hoping for a final sprint that, if successful, might give me the opportunity to change the U.S. Senate. Julia Roberts and Richard Gere were dining in his hotel room and beginning to fall in love when my iPhone signaled an incoming text.

"Just got initial results, and they don't look good for us," read Steve's message. "Give me a call and we can chat."

I phoned him back and learned that we were now at 10 percent. The result was devastating. We realized we had no chance to win. Having no wish to waste money or volunteers' time—or to give independent-minded voters false hope—I immediately stopped raising money, scaled back our staff, and canceled our campaign advertising. Once I knew I was going to lose, it didn't matter to me whether I finished with 24 percent or 4 percent. The race was effectively over. I would come to think of October 23 as my "real Election Day."

Although that day was the low point, my year of campaigning was a rewarding and enlightening experience. I developed a deep connection with the people of Maryland, many of whom had opened up to me about the struggles in their lives. I had no interest in doing the bidding of party bosses or special interest groups. I ran for office to bring our country together and to solve problems for the citizens of my state. And I never felt as passionately about anything I had done during my career.

While campaigning, I found that there is one political view that most voters share: our government is broken. To most people "broken" does not mean that their leaders hold ideological views different from their own. Instead, Marylanders expressed a belief that U.S. politics has become needlessly polarized and that our government is failing to address a host of important issues. This is true not only in my state. In 2019, the Gallup polling organization found that for the first time Americans of both parties view poor government as our greatest obstacle.[2] Confidence in our nation's ability to deal with either domestic or international issues has been "severely breached," Gallup found, and has reached record lows. Asked to rank the "most important problem facing the country today," nearly twice as many Americans named dysfunctional government as any other issue.[3]

Americans know our political system has been divided and debilitated, even if they aren't sure how and why it happened. Ordinary citizens might not have all the answers to the crisis at the United States-Mexico border, for example, but they can see that Democrats and Republicans would rather blame each other than work together to find a solution. They may realize that the Civil Rights Act (1964) and the Medicare Act (1965) passed with majorities of both parties, while the more recent Affordable Care Act (2010) and the Tax Cuts and Jobs Act (2017) went through without a single vote from the opposing party, but they don't know why compromise in Congress is now unreachable. They couldn't tell you how many confirmation votes Ruth Bader Ginsburg got in the Senate (ninety-six) or how many months Mitch McConnell blocked Barack Obama's replacement for Supreme Court Justice Antonin Scalia (fourteen), but they know the confirmation hearings for Justice Brett

Kavanaugh turned into an unruly political circus.

Average Americans aren't experts on political polarization. But they are certainly cognizant that our civic discourse has become uncivil, our governing institutions are ineffective, and the two dominant parties are under the thumb of hyperpartisan ideologues. Americans intuitively understand, as Harvard historian Jill Lepore wrote, "The more polarized its members, and the fewer the moderates, the less productive the Congress."[4]

When I ran for Senate, what I found was a system that benefits career politicians and challengers who are willing to court the base of one of the two major parties, but works in a hundred ways to undermine pragmatists who just want to serve their country. I confronted a duopolistic electoral system with onerous ballot requirements designed to block challenges from anyone other than the most partisan Democrats and Republicans. I campaigned in contorted congressional districts drawn to practically guarantee the success of select candidates, normally incumbents.

I encountered a rigged system in which independent voters are prevented from participating in the most important elections and party primaries relentlessly weed out moderate candidates. I discovered that incumbents control the way election debates work and how they manipulate the system to deny voters exposure to new candidates and fresh issues. I witnessed special interests funneling 90 percent of their funding to incumbents' campaigns[5], and I saw how they demand, in turn, that candidates pledge to support specific agendas.

Perhaps most depressing is that I found a political system built upon frenzied, angry fights, with little room for thoughtful or civil discourse. I encountered little interest in actual solutions that could gain bipartisan support. Instead of problem solving, political insiders were focused on the game—how to win and stay in power. Inside the

Washington Beltway, I repeatedly heard some variation of this: "Neal, you are right, but you cannot win this way."

The Fruits of Hyperpartisanship

We didn't get to this place overnight. The polarization warping U.S. politics can be traced to many historic factors, including the geographic self-sorting of Americans along political and cultural lines and a precipitous decline of objectivity in the mainstream media. These divisions in our society have been exacerbated by the rise of one-sided talk radio hosts, shout-fest cable TV, hyperpartisan Internet outlets, and social media echo chambers.

Moreover, the 1994 midterm elections changed the calculus for each party. Except for a two-year period during the first Eisenhower administration, the House had been safely in Democratic hands for as long as anyone on Capitol Hill could remember. Each party had more or less accepted this situation as the status quo. Suddenly, with the stunning GOP sweep, that model was altered, and both Democratic and Republican party strategists—and each party's activist base—began to treat each election cycle as a potential apocalypse. They feel that way because of the winner-take-all customs on Capitol Hill, where a single-seat margin translates into control of every committee, the legislative calendar, and the gavel in that body of Congress.

"We have a two-party system that the Founders didn't want, didn't envision, and tried to prevent—but which was nonetheless an inevitable result of the Constitution they wrote," says Brookings Institution political scientist William Galston. "Today, we have a government that is not only closely divided, but deeply divided. And we've learned that that's the worst of both worlds."[6]

The results can be seen in the following two sets of facts:

BREAKDOWN OF THE
U.S. ELECTORAL SYSTEM

Less than 10 percent of congressional general elections are considered competitive.[7]

The results of the other 90 percent of races are determined in a party primary by less than 20 percent of registered voters.[8]

The cost of elections rose from $1.7 billion in 2000, to $4.2 billion in 2016, and to $5.7 billion in 2018.[9]

In 2014, four years after the Supreme Court's decision in Citizens United, .001 percent of the population donated 29 percent of all political contributions.[10]

Incumbents get $9 in special interest money for every dollar that goes to a challenger.[11]

CONGRESS'S FAILING GRADES

The congressional approval rate is just 18 percent.[12]

Over the past seventy years, the share of congressmen and congresswomen who are moderates has fallen from 60 percent to just 12 percent.[13]

Over the same time period, the share of salient issues deadlocked in Congress has risen from about one in four to about three in four.[14]

The number of bills passed per congressional session has declined by half over the past forty years.[15]

Virtually *zero percent* of policy changes approved by Congress benefit the average American.[16]

The upshot is that Washington has become chronically incapable of solving problems. This is true, George Washington University political scientist Sarah A. Binder has shown, even on topics in which the outlines of a compromise are obvious and Americans have reached consensus.[17] Immigration and infrastructure are two examples where most Americans agree on a path, yet Congress cannot get anything done.

In fact, in the same Gallup poll showing a historic lack of confidence in government, the second biggest problem cited was immigration.[18] How Congress has dealt with this issue is a case study in political stalemate. Nearly everyone who has studied immigration believes the solution entails fortifying border security, forging a national consensus about *legal* immigration, modernizing procedures for those seeking entry as refugees (while housing them humanely), and implementing a path to citizenship for the millions of immigrants who have been here for years, especially those brought as children.

Long before Donald Trump vowed to build "a big beautiful wall" on the southern U.S. border, legislation that would have brought Americans what they want was derailed by right-wing Republicans and left-wing Democrats. It happened three times in a decade.

In May 2006, on a 62–36 vote, the Senate passed a compromise forged by Edward Kennedy and John McCain.[19] It called for increased border fencing, enhanced surveillance technology, and more border agents. It also expanded guest worker provisions and provided a path to citizenship for those who had lived here for many years. Although President George W. Bush praised the "bipartisan comprehensive reform," the bill never made it to his desk. Capitulating to opponents of amnesty, Republican House Speaker Dennis Hastert refused to bring it up for a vote. The House had passed its own comprehensive bill earlier, meaning a House-Senate Conference Committee could have been tasked with reconciling the two bills. No such committee was formed, however, and when the 109th Congress went out of session, the legislation expired.[20]

Two years later, another window of opportunity opened. In 2008, with the House in Democratic hands, Kennedy produced another bill, this time by working with Arizona's other Republican senator, Jon Kyl. Bucking the Senate's most liberal and conservative wings, Kennedy came up with just enough votes. At the eleventh hour, this fragile coalition was killed by a parliamentary trick known as a "poison pill." At the behest of organized labor, an amendment was offered to gut the bill's guest worker program. Its sponsors knew that adding this provision would make it impossible for most Republicans to support the bill. The poison pill amendment passed by one vote, with Democrats Hillary Clinton, Joe Biden, Bernie Sanders, and Barack Obama supporting it. As intended, it killed the legislation.

In 2013, the Senate approved a comprehensive plan developed by the Bipartisan Commission on Immigration Reform. But with Republicans back in control of the House, Speaker John Boehner wouldn't bring it to a vote. It had the votes to pass, but Boehner shelved it because a majority of Republican members weren't in favor.

Trump and his critics spent much of 2019 bickering over whether a "crisis" existed at the Mexican border. This was a frivolous argument. Whatever you call it, it's a serious problem that our politicians have failed to address for two decades. And it could have been resolved if they had been willing to work together.

Immigration is not an isolated example. Our political system is gridlocked on nearly every important policy issue we face. If our elected officials cannot put aside partisan concerns in areas where there is broad consensus, how can they tackle complicated issues such as gun violence, exorbitant healthcare costs, the burgeoning national debt, and a deteriorating education system? And is there any hope that we can address sweeping subjects such as income equality, climate change, and a dynamic global economy?

The answer is that, as long as we continue to reward hyperpartisan behavior, lawmakers will not solve these problems. For the most part, the men and women we send to Washington are not bad people. In my experience, they are likable folks who are simply responding to a perverse set of incentives.

"The problem is not Democrats or Republicans or the existence of parties *per se*. The problem is not individual politicians; most who seek and hold public office are genuinely seeking to make a positive contribution," Katherine M. Gehl and Michael E. Porter observed. "The real problem is the nature of competition in the politics industry."[21]

Gehl, a successful business executive, and Porter, a prominent Harvard Business School professor, wrote a much-acclaimed critique of U.S. politics that described a dysfunctional duopoly producing poor results for its customers, namely American citizens. "We need a new approach," they wrote. "Our political problems are not due to a single cause, but rather to a failure of the nature of the political competition that has been created. This is a systems problem."

To win elections, officeholders are forced into political corners where nothing gets done for the American people. They can't even pass a rational budget, which is why we're running $1 trillion peacetime deficits and accumulating a national debt that will cripple future generations. They can't approve presidential appointees in a timely manner and have trouble even keeping the government open. Partial shutdowns have become a regular feature of our politics, as though that were a normal way to run an enterprise. Lawmakers and presidents have closed national parks, stiffed government contractors, furloughed millions of federal employees, and caused havoc in the lives of citizens in standoffs over abortion, defense spending, and most recently—in the longest shutdown in U.S. history—over immigration policy. On most days, those on opposite sides of the aisle can't even have a civil conversation, let alone a good-faith negotiation that produces the reasonable legislative compromises the American people want and need for a functioning society.

Flipping the Narrative

In the early months of my campaign, I spoke to a group of sixty business leaders in the Dirksen Senate Office Building on Capitol Hill. This impressive edifice was named after Everett Dirksen, a moderate Republican from Illinois who served in the 1950s and 1960s as Senate minority leader. Dirksen was known for his ability to work constructively with Senate Democrats and presidents of either party. In a building named after this great statesman, I discussed the gradual breakdown of the U.S. Senate, once known as "the world's greatest deliberative body." One reason the Senate was held in esteem was men like Everett Dirksen, who not only knew how to forge compromise, but who never lost faith in the country and its representative form of government. American democracy, he was fond of saying, is like a waterlogged boat. "It moves slowly, it doesn't change direction quickly, but it never sinks."[22] I found myself wondering if we are moving at all these days and whether our ship remains unsinkable.

I'm hardly alone. "Our country is on a dangerous trajectory," Charles Wheelan, a Dartmouth University economist, wrote in *The Centrist Manifesto*, his call to action. "We are mired in serious policy challenges, in large part because the political process has moved beyond gridlock to complete paralysis."[23]

Wheelan conceptualized the "fulcrum strategy," which became an inspiration for my Senate run. Imagine electing a few independents—two or three might suffice—who would naturally ally themselves with the handful of Senate moderates from each party. In a closely divided Senate, this group would have the leverage to force changes in everything from improving the judicial confirmation process to passing comprehensive immigration legislation—and perhaps even choosing the Senate majority leader.

Charlie, who encouraged me to run for Senate, also founded Unite America, an organization working to strengthen our country's governance through its support of nonpartisan political reform initiatives. Other groups with similar aims have sprung to life, including Bridge Alliance, FairVote, Independent Voting, Issue One, Leadership Now, No Labels, RepresentUs, Stand Up Republic, the Bipartisan Policy Center, the National Association of Nonpartisan Reformers, and the Center for the Study of the Presidency and Congress.

Leadership Now estimates that $122 million is spent annually on reform efforts.[24] This sounds like a healthy figure, but it's a tiny fraction of the $56 billion spent on political activities by corporations, unions, the two major political parties, and various other interest groups.[25] Money is influence in Washington, and special interests and rich ideologues are outspending the rest of us 434 to 1.

By the way, when I say "us" in this book, I mean all Americans who are not part of the far right or the far left. Some of us are political independents. Some belong to third parties, such as the Libertarian Party or the burgeoning Alliance Party. Many of us consider ourselves moderate Democrats or Republicans—the kind of Americans who have a point of view, but who want a more effective government and who don't assume evil intent on the part of those who vote differently from us. We are the majority of Americans. We are not part of either party's polarized activist base, we don't contribute massive amounts of money to political campaigns, and we don't inundate our elected officials with angry missives.

But we need to get involved, and now is the time. A critical mass of Americans knows that what we have is broken. As you will see in the pages that follow, we have some momentum on a number of reform efforts to fix the system. These opportunities don't come along often. It's been almost three decades since Ross Perot ran as an independent candidate for president and tapped into widespread voter dissatisfaction. While things in Washington are much worse today, the good news is that more people realize it.

Thousands of would-be reformers have joined over one hundred groups. Although these pages will relate some of my experiences as a candidate challenging the two-party system for a seat at the table, this contract is about something far greater than a single campaign. This book is intended as a rallying point and a guide for those of us working to restore the soaring promise of democratic self-government.

Contract to Unite America lays out a set of ideas—some original, many conceived by my fellow reformers—that would reshape the incentives in our political system. In 1994, Republicans upended conventional wisdom by winning a majority of the House of Representatives for the first time in four decades. Part of the GOP's campaign arsenal that year was Newt Gingrich's famed "Contract with America." As political theater, it was ingenious and effective. As a blueprint for change, it was something less than that: a litany of pet projects Republican Party bosses had been proposing for years. What America really needs are reforms, passed on a bipartisan basis, that change how politics is conducted in this country.

Six of the items in my contract would counteract distortions to our system that have nearly guaranteed the election of partisan extremists. These items range from how candidates qualify for ballots to how elections are run. Two additional items deal with campaign finance law—they would require transparency and limit the ability of corporations, special interests, and oligarchs to outspend everyone else. Two others would encourage better behavior in our elected officials after they arrive in Washington. Every one of these ideas, polls show, is favored by at least 60 percent of Americans.

None of the items in my contract would be enough by itself to fix our broken system, but each one would make a difference, and together they would rejuvenate American democracy. Can it be done? The political realist in me admits to harboring doubts. But the romantic in me believes in happy endings, like in *Pretty Woman*. In that Hollywood fairy tale, Richard Gere's Edward, the wealthy businessman who rescues Julia Roberts's Vivian character, must conquer his fear of heights to scale the castle (actually, a fire escape) to save our heroine. Vivian, in her own words, "rescues him right back."

It's time for Americans to save each other. At the least, we need to learn how to work together again for the common good. We've done it before, at times that also strained the bonds of our affection. In his last speech, Senator John McCain lamented the result of forgetting this lesson.

"We are getting nothing done, my friends," McCain said. "We're getting nothing done."[26]

That can change. Yes, it's true that we now have a system dominated by a duopolistic political elite accomplishing very little for the American people. But it's also true that Americans know the system is broken and they want to fix it. And I present you a plan.

The Contract to Unite America

As citizens, we believe our government is divided and ineffective. Our elected leaders have not taken essential policy steps regarding education, immigration, infrastructure, job creation, healthcare costs, and our national debt, to name a few.

Washington, D.C., has been reconfigured by partisan insiders to benefit their parties and funding allies. Our political system incentivizes divisiveness and gridlock rather than practical solutions to our nation's pressing challenges.

To counteract today's destructive hyperpartisanship, we need fewer rigid ideologues and more pragmatic representatives willing to collaborate for the common good. We need more legislation passed on a bipartisan basis. We need more action, especially when a majority agrees on an issue. And we need more civility. As Abraham Lincoln said in his first inaugural address, "We must not be enemies. Though passion may have strained, it must not break our bonds of affection."

We want to be proud of the way free people govern themselves. In that spirit, we propose the following measures:

1. **Open Primaries Act:** Every publicly financed election, including primary elections, will be open to all registered voters, regardless of party affiliation.

2. **Educated Electorate Act:** A nonpartisan Federal Debate Commission will be created to ensure the fairness and caliber of presidential and congressional election debates.

3. **Term Limits Constitutional Amendment:** Members of the U.S. House of Representatives will be limited to three terms of two years. Members of the U.S. Senate will be limited to two terms of six years.

4. **Elections Transparency Act:** For any contribution of $100 or more to any candidate, party, or political entity, the donor's identity must be disclosed publicly.

5. **Campaign Finance Constitutional Amendment:** Government may distinguish between corporations and people, and Congress and the states can apply reasonable limits on campaign spending.

6. **Ballot Access Act:** To be included on an election ballot, all candidates will be subject to identical requirements, which cannot exceed five thousand signatures on a petition.

7. **Fair Districts Act:** Each state will form an independent commission responsible for redistricting. Political affiliation can no longer be considered when drawing districts.

8. **Fair Representation Act:** Ranked-choice voting will be used in federal elections, and states with more than one member in the House of Representatives will create multimember districts of up to five members.

9. **Congressional Rules:** Procedures in the House and Senate will be altered to reduce the power of the ideological fringes and encourage bipartisan legislation and cooperation.

10. **Creating a Culture of Unity:** We call on our next president to form a bipartisan administration, for Congress to sign a civility pledge, for Americans to participate in national service, and for our schools to revive civics education.

Collectively these actions will help create a republic that lives up to the promise of America's founding. We ask our fellow citizens as free and independent people to champion these reforms and pledge their names to this Contract to Unite America.

Contract Item 1

OPEN PRIMARIES ACT:

Every publicly financed election, including primary elections, will be open to all registered voters, regardless of party affiliation.

Let My People Vote

On June 26, 2018, the top government job in my county went to a candidate chosen by fewer than 6 percent of the registered voters. I live in Montgomery County, Maryland, where our 1.1 million residents make us the state's most populous county. We are a "majority minority" jurisdiction (45 percent non-Hispanic white) with a diverse economy that includes many federal government jobs. Montgomery County is also 60 percent Democratic, with the remaining registered voters divided fairly evenly between Republicans and independents. What this means is that when choosing our elected officeholders, the only contests that matter are Democratic Party primaries.

The 2018 primary for county executive, the highest office in county government, was a hotly contested race among six well-qualified candidates. Marc Elrich was a highly progressive, twelve-year veteran of the county council. David Blair, an entrepreneur from the health benefits industry, was a moderate who ran on a platform of job creation. The other four were: Roger Berliner, another twelve-year member of the county council who represented some of the wealthiest parts of the county; Bill Frick, a member of Maryland's House of Delegates; Rose Krasnow, the former mayor of Rockville, the county seat; and George Leventhal, a third member of the county council, who had served as a longtime legislative aide to Democratic lawmakers in Annapolis and Washington, D.C.

After the ballots were tallied and a mandatory recount done, Elrich won the six-way race with 37,532 votes compared to Blair's 37,455. In November, Elrich would easily win the general election with 65 percent of the vote. As usual, the Democratic primary was the real election. Our county's highest-ranking elected official had been chosen by the relatively small group of Democratic activists who showed up to vote in a non-presidential-year primary. These are Montgomery County's most liberal voters. Most moderate Democrats did not vote, and independents and Republicans were not permitted to vote.

Such outcomes make a mockery of self-government. The Maryland Democratic Party's closed primary rules prohibit Republican participation and flatly disenfranchise the 22 percent of Montgomery County who are independent voters, with predictable consequences. Had independents been permitted to vote, it's not a certainty that the more moderate David Blair would have won. But it seems highly likely to me. Blair lost to Elrich by only seventy-seven votes. With over 146,000 unaffiliated voters in the county, wouldn't Blair have easily made up the difference? We'll never know for sure, but I know this much: he'd have made up three of them in my household alone.

Getting "Closed Primaried"

The Montgomery County elections of 2018 were not an aberration. Nationally, few congressional races are competitive in the general election. According to the Government Affairs Institute at Georgetown University, the trend toward fewer competitive House districts is true over the past twenty years, the past fifty years, and even over the past one hundred years.[1] Today, fewer than 10 percent of races are decided by less than a 5 percent margin. In closed primaries where one party has a sizable advantage over the other, independents are barred from the only elections that actually matter.

In twenty-one states, at least one of the two major political parties holds closed primaries for either presidential or congressional elections or both. In ten of them (Connecticut, Delaware, Florida, Kentucky, Maryland, Nevada, New Mexico, New York, Oregon, and Pennsylvania), both parties have closed primaries for all federal elections. The upshot is that millions of Americans are effectively prohibited from having a voice in who represents them at every level of government. Twenty-six million independent voters—the fastest-growing segment—stand to be excluded from the 2020 presidential race.[2]

A recent example of how closed primaries warp U.S. politics occurred in the 2018 Democratic primary in New York's Fourteenth Congressional District. There, ten-term incumbent Joseph Crowley faced a little-known challenger named Alexandria Ocasio-Cortez. A waitress who had volunteered for Bernie Sanders's presidential campaign in 2016, she remained active in progressive causes after that election. Crowley was an experienced lawmaker—and quite liberal in his own right. A harsh critic of President Trump's immigration policies and supporter of Medicare for All, Crowley had received a 94 percent rating from the League of Conservation Voters,[3] and 100 percent ratings from NARAL and Planned Parenthood, both of which endorsed him.[4] Crowley had also risen to become the fourth-highest-ranking Democrat in the House and had chaired the House Democratic Caucus. None of it was enough.

In his safely Democratic district, Crowley had been reelected nine times without facing a serious primary opponent. This time, despite his own progressive *bona fides*, he found himself a member of the wrong gender, wrong ethnic group, and wrong generation in a New York City district where he could be attacked with impunity from the left by a twenty-eight-year old member of the Democratic Socialists of America. Putting her Bernie Sanders connections to work, Ocasio-Cortez advocated for free public college, a federal jobs guarantee, a Green New Deal, and the abolishment of the Immigration and Customs Enforcement. What made her candidacy even remotely viable was the fact that, in this nearly monolithic Democratic district, all she needed to do was win a low-turnout primary featuring thirty thousand of the district's most liberal voters. Ocasio-Cortez ran a grassroots campaign with a highly progressive message, raised enough money in small donations to compete, and in a district with nearly seven hundred thousand residents won the primary by attracting only 16,898 votes. She captured a U.S. House seat with votes from only 4.8 percent of her district's registered voters—in an election that excluded Republicans and independents.

In the parlance of politics, Joe Crowley had been "primaried." But perhaps a better way to think of it is that he had been "closed primaried."

Principled Neutrality

The rationale used to defend voting restrictions that produce such results is that political parties are formed to advance policy agendas and have the right to choose their own candidates. This explanation has superficial logic, but it would carry more weight if elections weren't sponsored, overseen, and financed by government. In other words, if the parties want to behave like private organizations advancing a policy agenda, then let them pay for their own election activities. As an independent, I should not be required to pay for election activities in which I cannot participate. This amounts to taxation without representation, one of the grievances that helped create this country.

Defenders of the entrenched system have a simple retort: if you want to participate in a primary, then register with one of the two major parties. But it's not that simple. What they are really saying is that if you want to participate in the only meaningful election, you must register with the majority party in your jurisdiction, irrespective of your views. As an independent, I've always found this troubling. But unless they live in competitive congressional districts or swing states, Republicans and Democrats face the same dilemma wherever they are in the minority. In Joe Crowley's district, independents should be allowed to vote in the Democratic primary. So should Republicans. That's how it works in the twenty-three states where any registered voter can cast a ballot in any primary for federal office.

During my Senate campaign, in a one-hour discussion aired on Baltimore's NPR station, interviewer Tom Hall asked me what was wrong with closed primaries. I replied that if the parties want to operate as private organizations and exclude huge swaths of voters, then they should finance their own elections. But if they depend upon government funding for their activities, all voters should be permitted to participate. These costs are not trivial: a study done two years ago by an organization called Open Primaries estimated that it cost $288 million in the closed primary states alone.[5]

This is about more than money, however. Declining to join either of these two parties is, for millions of Americans, a matter of principle. It certainly is for me. Why should I have to join an organization that promotes policies I oppose—and for me that means the Democratic Party and the GOP—to fully participate in the civic life of my country?

I have been a registered independent most of my adult life. It's part of my identity. When I grew up, my mother was a Democrat, and my father a Republican. My mother is an immigrant from Morocco, who arrived in the United States at age eighteen. She became a Democrat mainly because of the party's inclusiveness of immigrant communities, regardless of race, ethnicity, or religion. My father's parents were immigrants from Belarus, who, like my mother's family, came to this country because they felt it was a place where you could work hard and get ahead. Dad lived it too. I grew up watching him work six days a week, and he still believes in the importance of a strong work ethic, as do his children.

My parents also fostered and encouraged independence. I rode my bicycle everywhere, including soccer practices, and sometimes an hour to the beach. We were encouraged to think for ourselves. Someone once asked me what one childhood message I remember most from my father, and I responded: "Let him make his own decisions."

When I turned eighteen, I promptly registered to vote as an independent. Even then, when the two major parties were less polarized and less ideologically extreme than today, I never agreed entirely with either one. I shared the Republicans' belief in personal responsibility, respect for the private sector, and willingness to realistically factor the economic costs of taxation and regulation. I shared conservatives' skepticism that government programs are the best answer for all of society's problems. But I also appreciated Democrats' emphasis on social tolerance, commitment to a strong social safety net, and concern about the environment. As Republicans moved further right, I broke company with them on issues ranging from gun violence to climate change and questioned why the party of small government wants to regulate behavior in Americans' bedrooms.

In other words, I am a true independent. My first presidential vote was for George H. W. Bush. At the time, in 1988, I was a student at Brown University and placed a Bush for President sign in my dorm room window. Twenty years later, I voted for Barack Obama. In 2014, I split my ticket in Maryland, voting on the same day for Democratic county executive Ike Leggett and Republican governor Larry Hogan.

Before running for the U.S. Senate, my only previous campaigns for elective office were in the early 1980s at George W. Hewlett High School on Long Island, where I was elected class president three times. A reasonably athletic kid, I was a better math student.* During my childhood, family was a focus. We have a large family, and our typical holiday gatherings included some seventy people, with conversations in three or four languages. Many of those family members would become supporters of my campaign, as were many childhood friends.

These days I live in a county where the only elections that count are the Democratic primaries. That got old, and in 2005, I registered as a Democrat so I could vote in their closed primaries. It was a compromise that wasn't satisfying, and in 2011, I was reminded why. That year, Democrats turned their backs on the recommendations of the Simpson-Bowles commission. Co-chaired by Republican Alan Simpson and Democrat Erskine Bowles and formally known as the National Commission on Fiscal Responsibility and Reform, the commission fashioned a bipartisan plan to address our soaring annual federal budget deficits. The eighteen-member commission was split between Democrats and Republicans, and its recommendations were thoughtful and thorough. The plan took aim at each party's sacred cows. Republicans compromised on defense spending and revenue increases. Democrats accepted cuts to entitlements and some cherished items in the discretionary budget.

In the months after the recommendations were made, I watched with dismay as President Obama and Democratic congressional leaders ignored a wise and bipartisan solution. I reregistered as an independent, which in Maryland is called "unaffiliated."

---

* My three kids like to say that they "are athletes, and Dad was a *mathlete*."

Subverting Reform

An alternative way to look at Americans who choose to affiliate with neither major party is that these are consumers who are being failed by the market—in this case, the marketplace of ideas.

We live in a country of 330 million people who are somehow supposed to be shoehorned into only two political classifications. American customers can choose among dozens of smartphones, a hundred different kinds of cars, five hundred cable stations. Yet, we're all supposed to be highly partisan conservative Republicans or liberal Democrats. Worse, we're expected to accept this binary choice even as those two parties stampede madly toward their respective ideological extremes.

Until the turn of the twentieth century, party nominees were chosen in a caucus setting,* sometimes even in those infamous "smoke filled rooms."[6] Along came the famous reformers of the day, many of them liberal Republicans who became Progressive Party leaders, men such as Theodore Roosevelt, Robert M. La Follette of Wisconsin, and Hiram Johnson of California.[7] Their antidote was direct primaries, which Progressives saw as a way to counter special interests and corrupt party bosses who controlled the caucuses. Seeking to break the stranglehold held by the Southern Pacific Railroad on lawmakers in Sacramento, Johnson and his fellow California reformers also introduced mechanisms to recall officeholders with a straight majority vote, to use a referendum process to enact laws or amend the state's constitution, and to eliminate party affiliations on the ballot.[8]

---

* Respected social commentator Jonathan Rauch wrote a provocative 2016 *Atlantic* essay arguing that the absence of "smoke filled" rooms where party bosses forged compromise has created a political vacuum. I wouldn't go that far, but I agree with Rauch's main thesis, which is that what is taking place today isn't "a spasm" of chaos, but rather, "a chaos *syndrome*."

In rapid succession, similar reforms swept the West and Midwest. Direct primary elections were adopted in all but a handful of states. "The direct primary…takes away the power of the party leader or boss and places the responsibility for control upon the individual," said Senator George W. Norris of Nebraska. "It lessens party spirit and decreases partisanship."[9]

That was the idea, but the system always fights back.

In California, the epicenter of the good-government movement, reformers deleted party identification from the ballot altogether. This proved to be a bridge too far. It gave entrenched politicians a way to subvert the new primary system. That ploy was exacerbated by another innovation known as "cross-filing," a mechanism where candidates can seek the nomination of more than one party. Still used in New York today, cross-filing was introduced to California in 1914. In Sacramento, the result was that incumbents became virtually invincible. Republicans retained control of state government for decades—as voters literally didn't know the party identification of the candidates on the general election ballot.[10]

By the 1950s, Democrats and grassroots citizen groups were demanding change. They were essentially tweaking the excesses and unintended consequences of the Progressive Era. Weakening the parties, to the degree that happened in California, only empowered the special interests. So cross-filing was abolished, political identifications were put back on the ballot, and parties were allowed to close their primaries.

But in closing primaries, these second-generation reformers made the same mistake as their Progressive Era forefathers: they undermined their own good intentions. Over time, closed primaries aided and abetted the process of the stronger party maintaining its dominance.[11]

Today party chieftains may resist letting millions of moderates participate in their party elections, but common sense tells you that it would make their party grow—and make Americans less negative about politics. Clearly, most voters favor opening primaries. A January 2019 poll of Florida voters found that 70 percent of those surveyed support opening primaries to independents.[12] This *should* appeal to both liberals (who insist that they want every person to vote) as well as conservatives who profess fealty to America's Founding Fathers.

The founders did not envision or desire a government controlled by two parties. The Constitution was written with the idealistic assumption that our elected leaders would work together to find common ground—as they did in Philadelphia to produce the revered document. The Constitution itself makes no reference to political parties, and a number of the framers openly expressed the fear that Americans might develop more loyalty to "factions" (i.e., political parties) than to their country. George Washington was one of those who sounded the call most clearly.[13] Politically independent himself, Washington warned in his farewell address as president about the danger of an environment characterized by "the alternate domination of one faction over another, sharpened by the spirit of revenge."

This wasn't a strictly theoretical concern. Political parties were already forming. Today, the very nightmare George Washington described is the defining feature of our civic life. In stark contrast to the ideals of our Founding Fathers, modern leaders of the Republican and Democratic parties behave as if the government belongs to them.

In January 2019, when Howard Schultz announced that he was considering running for president as an independent, he was savaged by Democratic Party leaders. They reacted as though the mere possibility he might siphon support from the Democrats' 2020 nominee was a crime against nature. Thirty seconds into Schultz's first campaign event in New York City, one attendee yelled "Don't help elect Trump, you egotistical, billionaire asshole!"[14]

The mainstream media added fuel to the fire, urging Schultz not to run. All this happened before anything was known about his policy positions or vision of America's future. Instead, Democrats attacked him for potentially "spoiling" the 2020 election. The media concurred with this story line, focusing on the horse race, not the horse. In a nutshell, their argument is that Schultz's candidacy should depend upon his ability to win a primary election of the country's most liberal voters.

In response, Greg Orman and I co-authored an opinion piece for the *Wall Street Journal* defending Schultz's right to run.[15] Americans unaffiliated with any party have just as much right to seek office as those with *D*'s or *R*'s by their names. Moreover, since the current duopoly is producing such bad results for our country, you'd think they would be more modest about attacking someone who promised a different approach.

It's Not Party Time

A number of prominent citizens share the founders' concerns and crave something better than the partisan, ineffective government we have now. I was fortunate to be included in a group of some two dozen such people who met in Philadelphia in August 2017, before I had decided to run for office. Among the attendees were: Greg Orman; Alaska governor Bill Walker; Craig O'Dear, who would run for U.S. Senate in Missouri; Charles Wheelan, author of *The Centrist Manifesto*; Bill Kristol, editor of *The Weekly Standard*; Michael Smerconish, CNN host; Matthew Dowd, former George W. Bush aide; Evan McMullin, 2016 independent presidential candidate; John Avlon, political commentator; and Nick Troiano, executive director of Unite America.

The group discussed whether we should become a third party or remain a movement. We decided that our role model was not the Libertarian Party or the Green Party, but something more similar to Emmanuel Macron's En Marche movement in France. We were fortunate to be joined for one session by Aziz-François Ndiaye, a key member of the campaign team that had engineered Macron's victory in France's 2017 presidential election. Ndiaye explained that Macron viewed political parties as part of the problem and deliberately created a movement that would feel welcoming to previous members of any party.

I modeled my campaign on this concept. Frequently asked why we did not start a third party, I would respond by saying, "I am part of a movement of Democrats, Republicans, and independents who believe our country needs to come together, change the way Washington works, and put the interests of Maryland ahead of the interests of any political parties."

Along the way, I concluded that a significant first step would be empowering *all* voters to participate in any taxpayer-funded election, including primaries. Political scientists talk about "open" primaries, "semi-open" primaries, "semi-closed" primaries, and "closed primaries." My position is simple: the more open, the better. Totally open is best.

In Virginia, citizens are registered to vote—not as Republicans or Democrats, but as citizens. Under the law, everyone is essentially an independent: on primary day, they show up at the polls and are offered a ballot to vote in either the Republican or Democratic primary—and vote accordingly. Texas, Colorado, and Minnesota have similar systems.

Even in states with party registration, however, I believe Republicans should be able to vote in Democratic primaries and vice versa. This already happens in twenty-three states. Some partisan leaders complain that this gives party activists the chance to wreak havoc in the opposing party's primary. But this kind of mischief is rare, and for me it's a minor concern compared to excluding huge portions of our voters from the only election that matters.

Another method to give every citizen a voice is to have all voters participate in the same primary, a system called a "blanket" primary or "jungle" primary. California and Washington state have adopted jungle primaries where the top two finishers move on to the general election, regardless of party affiliation. A variation on jungle primaries, supported by many reformers including myself, is "top four," which gives general election voters exposure to an even wider range of candidates and ideas.* Had either method been used in New York's Fourteenth Congressional District, for instance, the two top finishers still would have been Alexandria Ocasio-Cortez and Joe Crowley. They would have met again in November. With Republican and independents' participation, Crowley likely would have been reelected, and we might have all forgotten AOC's name by now.

Expand and Protect

Item 1 of the Contract to Unite America, the Open Primaries Act, mandates the inclusion of all voters in any taxpayer-funded election, regardless of their party affiliation. Beyond this requirement, consistent with Article 1 Section 5 of the U.S. Constitution, it would be up to the states to manage the details.

Fortunately, most of the country already has open primaries. Of the states still with closed primaries, more than half are controlled by Democrats. This helps explain why opening primaries was not included in the Democrats' ambitious, but partisan, political reform bill H.R. 1, which was introduced in Congress in early 2019.

---

* We may get an electoral test of it in 2020, as Alaskans for Better Elections are pursuing a statewide referendum on top-four balloting.

In some of the remaining states, reformers are beginning to make headway. In Colorado, Kent J. Thiry, a local healthcare executive, headed up a bipartisan organization, "Let Colorado Vote," that drafted Proposition 108, taking aim at the state's closed primary system. The need was particularly acute in Colorado, where registered independent voters outnumber Republicans and Democrats. In November 2016, the voters sent a strong message to the duopoly: Proposition 108 was passed.

"This is a big win for democracy in Colorado," said Thiry. "Colorado's voters have proven once again the wisdom of government of the people, by the people and for the people."[16]

But a reformer's work is never done. In fashioning statutory language to implement the new procedures, the legislature inserted provisions requiring independents to publicly declare a party preference. "By declaring a preference, you really become an affiliated voter," noted Kelly Brough, a Denver business leader who worked with Let Colorado Vote. "I don't think that's what voters said they wanted in November."[17]

Meanwhile a group named Open Primaries has been leading the fight against rearguard actions by lawmakers to close primaries in Missouri, Wyoming, and Tennessee, where they are currently open.

"Reform must not simply be enacted, it must be completed," Open Primaries founder John Opdycke told me. "When the playing field is leveled, the citizenry has to grab the opportunity to play in new ways. Otherwise, the same old forces, the same old patterns will adapt to the new rules and politics as usual will reassert itself."[18]

As if on cue, in Missouri, Republican state representative Dan Stacy sponsored an egregious bill that requires voters to be assigned to a specific political party for a full year before being allowed to vote in a primary.[19] Moderate Democrats and Republicans raised concerns, but as this once purple swing state has become dependably Republican red, GOP leaders have sought a partisan advantage. Missouri Republican representative Sheila Solon, for one, thinks her party went too far.

"We're going to disenfranchise people who consider themselves independent," she said while the legislation was being debated in March 2019.[20] That's the very idea, as Solon knows from personal experience. She lost a bruising primary to Dan Stacy in 2016, in a district so conservative that there was no Democratic nominee to face in November. Solon regained a seat in the legislature by moving to another district in 2018, but Stacy doesn't want to risk losing his seat to any challenger. He essentially wants to restrict the electorate in a way that virtually guarantees the election of far-right conservatives in his district and in other districts like it.

"We want people who have a vested interest in Republican principles to vote for Republicans," explained Jered Taylor, another conservative Missouri lawmaker who signed on to Stacy's bill. "We want people with a vested interested in Democrat principles to vote for Democrats."[21]

I couldn't have said it any better myself. That's exactly what Missouri Republican bosses want, and it's what Democratic elites want in heavily "blue" states. And it's exactly what's wrong with American politics.

All Votes Matter

Closed primaries are an apt metaphor for closed minds. The duopoly's mind-set puts Americans in boxes. It typecasts minority voters and alienates young voters. Dr. Jesse Fields, an African American physician I met in Nashville at the Unrig Summit, believes that treating entire ethnic groups as monolithic voting blocs is a perversion of the civil rights movement, not its natural outcome.

"That the black community would become a foregone conclusion as the constituency of any political party was not the mission of those who marched for civil rights," Dr. Fields maintains.[22] A board member for Open Primaries, she added, "Opening the primaries and independent redistricting are key to true minority enfranchisement because they give all voters, including the millions of minority voters who are independent, equal voting rights, the actual freedom to vote for who they choose to rather than the party dictating the choices."

You know who gets this? Young Americans, now our nation's largest generational cohort. Although they skew liberal,[23] 44 percent of millennials describe themselves as independents, more than for any of the nation's older voting blocs.[24] This trend is even more pronounced among the nation's very youngest demographic group—the Gen Zers born after 1996.[25] In some key states, about half of them are rejecting both the Democrats and the Republicans when registering to vote.[26]

During the writing of this book, my youngest child, Sophie, turned sixteen and a half and got her driver's license. In Maryland, the Department of Motor Vehicles preregisters young people to vote when they get their license. Although Sophie won't be eligible to vote until she turns eighteen, she'll do so in time to vote for the presidential election of 2020. When she came home from the DMV, she showed me the paperwork which included her party registration—as unaffiliated.

I would have been proud of her no matter what registration she chose, but I can't lie: it was pleasing that she chose to be an independent. A father's pride was diminished, however, by the knowledge that I live in a place where the adults in power don't really want her to vote in the elections that matter.

That must change.

Contract Item 2

EDUCATED ELECTORATE ACT:

A nonpartisan Federal Debate Commission will be created to ensure the fairness and caliber of presidential and congressional election debates.

Designing Better Debates

On Sunday, October 7, 2018, at 3:00 p.m., in the studio of Fox 45 in Baltimore, I participated in a televised debate with Senator Cardin and Republican challenger Tony Campbell. The moderator was Jennifer Gilbert, a TV anchor for Baltimore's *WBFF News*. In some ways, this experience was the high point of my campaign. The feedback from viewers was overwhelmingly positive. They felt I came across likable, trustworthy, and substantive on the issues. Shortly afterward, we peaked in the polls at 18 percent.

During the debate, I focused on issues on which the majority of Americans supported moderate solutions, but where the two parties held more extreme positions. On immigration, for example, I questioned Cardin about his party's hostility to the Immigration and Customs Enforcement Agency (ICE), while condemning Campbell for his advocacy of policies that tear apart immigrant families. I called for a compromise that included improving border security and establishing a path to citizenship for law-abiding, tax-paying residents who have been in the United States for many years.

Likewise, I took a middle ground on healthcare, saying that the nation's focus should be on improving the Affordable Care Act. I chided Campbell for advocating the repeal of the ACA without offering any replacement, which would leave millions of Americans uninsured. I also questioned Cardin for supporting Medicare for All, which would entail a massive expansion of the federal government.

I pointed out that Cardin marches in lockstep with Senate Democratic Leader Chuck Schumer. Cardin voted with his party's leadership 97 percent of the time, more than any other senator. In response to a question about the greatest threat to our country, I answered: "President Trump's Twitter account and Senator Cardin's rubber stamp."

Near the end, I asked the audience to imagine the history books our children and grandchildren will read in the future. I described a chapter called "Partisanship and Divisiveness" covering the 1990s to 2010s and then asked people to imagine the next chapter, one in which the country comes together and moves forward. I asked them to join a movement of Democrats, Republicans, and independents—and to vote for someone who will represent the people of Maryland rather than a political party. At the end of the debate, I challenged my opponents to two more debates, and said that I'd meet them "anytime, anywhere."[1]

Yet this session, watched by only 1 percent of Maryland voters, would be the campaign's only debate. This was by design, the design of the incumbent, who didn't perform well that day and didn't want to risk his front-runner status. The small audience was no accident either. Our debate was held during a Baltimore Ravens game in the middle of a three-day weekend. This was the only time slot Cardin's camp would accept. Worse, despite previously agreeing to a second televised debate, Cardin refused to make good on his word.

Democracy Is Dying in Darkness

How did Ben Cardin get away with this?

If you are like me, you probably assume that standards exist for campaign debates for the United States Senate. There must be rules about who gets to participate, when the debates happen, how many are scheduled, when they are broadcast, who chooses the moderator, what the format will look like, and which topics will be covered.

The truth is that there are almost no standards for debates. In each election, the teams negotiate and only if they agree does a debate even take place. Debates have become one more tool used by the parties to manipulate our electoral system. Incumbents have a built-in advantage, since they already have the name identification and record on which to run. In 2018, 84 percent of Senate incumbents won. Two years earlier it was 93 percent.

During my election cycle in 2018, there were thirty-five U.S. Senate races. In fifteen of them, there was either no debate or only one debate. The most common explanation for why the public was provided so little exposure to the candidates facing off against each other was that the leading candidate, normally the incumbent, was too "busy." This is an insult to the voters' intelligence.

In my case, once Cardin decided that further debates would only hurt his chances of reelection, he refused to schedule another one. Tony Campbell's performance was even weaker. So he didn't really want another debate either. We contacted Cardin's team multiple times by phone, email, and letter, but they were committed to preventing Marylanders from seeing the seventy-five-year-old senator in action.

We tried to force the issue through the media, but my faith in that institution proved misplaced. In the prior few months, the *Washington Post* and the *Baltimore Sun*, our region's largest papers, as well as the newspaper in the state capital,[2] had written several articles about the scheduling of the gubernatorial debates between Republican incumbent Larry Hogan and Democratic challenger Ben Jealous. The *Sun* even wrote a piece quoting experts critical of the governor for not scheduling more than one debate. "It's a shame for Maryland voters," said Mileah Kromer, director of the Sarah T. Hughes Field Politics Center at Goucher College. The candidates "need to step back and recognize that this is a function that campaigns serve for American democracy."[3]*

If those two newspapers applied consistent editorial standards, it would put pressure on Cardin to come out of hiding. Unfortunately, the *Post* and the *Sun* treated the Senate race differently. They simply wouldn't write about it.

The *Washington Post* would go on to endorse Cardin without ever meeting me. Even when I polled more strongly than every unaffiliated and third-party Senate candidate in the country, neither the *Post* nor the *Sun* would give my campaign much coverage. After the election, I was asked, "What was the greatest disappointment of my campaign?" Without hesitation, I said, "The *Washington Post*." †

I had read that newspaper nearly every day for twenty-eight years and was saddened by the bias it exhibited throughout the campaign. The *Post*'s defenders might point out that I ended up with less than 4 percent of the vote. But this is looking at it backward. The *Post* wouldn't cover our campaign even when I was polling at 18 percent. As political writers

---

* A columnist for the *Capital Gazette* in Annapolis chided incumbents for scheduling debates when hardly anyone would see them live. My appreciation was tempered, however, by the sole reference to me as "Neal Smith."

† The question about the greatest disappointment of my campaign was asked at a twenty-person dinner party organized by a friend. I realized after I responded that next to me was Steve Hills, the former president of the *Washington Post*. Steve was disappointed in my response but knew I was being honest. We have become closer friends in the past year.

and editors know full well, a campaign can't catch fire if ordinary voters aren't aware of what it stands for and what its candidate is doing. Contrary to their slogan, during my campaign, the *Washington Post* seemed quite willing to allow democracy to die in darkness.

Debating Is as American as Apple Pie

Although no written record exists of the first political debates on these shores, it's likely that they took place in Dorchester, Massachusetts, in 1633. In that settlement, exactly 150 years before Great Britain formally ceased hostilities in the Revolutionary War, the first town hall meeting convened in the colonies.[4] Questions of self-government were brought up, voted on, and honored as law. The custom caught on and took root throughout New England, highlighting two principles that would form the basis of American self-government: open debate and majority rule.

In *The Federalist Papers*, James Madison outlines the rationale for direct election of House members in words that practically demand public debate. "As it is essential to liberty that the government in general, should have a common interest with the people," Madison wrote, "so it is particularly essential that the [House of Representatives] should have an immediate dependence on, & intimate sympathy with the people."[5]

Madison was defending the practice of holding House elections every two years. How was such "intimate sympathy" to be achieved and maintained? By mingling with constituents, debating opponents, and standing regularly for reelection. Public debates were so integral to this process that ducking them was considered bad form—and could sink an incumbent. That's how Democrats loyal to Andrew Jackson torpedoed the political career of Davy Crockett.

Yes, the future Disney hero who died heroically at the Alamo was a politician in this country's early days. Along with Henry Clay, he was an early practitioner of the "stump speech," the progenitor of the campaign debate.[6] After Crockett opposed President Andrew Jackson's harsh policies toward the Cherokees and other Native American tribes, Jackson's allies went after Crockett. In his autobiography, Crockett explained how his adversaries spread word (without Crockett's knowledge) that a debate would be held in some backwoods Tennessee town where Crockett would be called upon to defend his opposition to Jackson. Because Crockett was never informed of these "debates," he didn't show up.[7]

Notwithstanding the fact that Crockett was the victim of a dirty trick, his campaign was dealt a fatal blow because avoiding debates was considered cowardly. In those days—unlike in my 2018 race—an incumbent who ducked a challenger paid a steep price for it. Crockett lost his congressional seat.*

In 1858, an Illinois Senate race made campaign debates more or less a permanent part of the American political landscape when Senator Stephen A. Douglas and challenger Abraham Lincoln engaged in what became known as the Great Debates. This appellation certainly fit. The subject they were debating was nothing less than the future of slavery. Moreover, these face-offs helped solidify Lincoln's future as an 1860 national candidate and launch the upstart Republican Party itself.

But then, a depressingly familiar impulse asserted itself. Although the Lincoln-Douglas debates were extraordinary, once the Republican Party displaced the Whig Party, the new duopoly exerted its pernicious influence. Typically, the incumbent would refuse to debate the

---

* You could also say that Davy Crockett paid for the perception that he'd skipped debates with his life. Three months after telling his former Tennessee colleagues that they "could go to hell and I would go to Texas," Crockett lay dead at The Alamo, along with all the other defenders of the mission.

challenger. This impulse has been hard to combat.

Although twentieth century communications technologies created an opportunity for Americans to see democracy in action, the leaders of the two major parties haven't always welcomed them. In 1940, President Franklin Roosevelt declined Wendell Willkie's offer for a series of radio debates.[8] President Dwight Eisenhower refused Adlai Stevenson's offer to debate on television in 1956.[9]

It would be one hundred years after the Lincoln-Douglas debate before two presidential nominees would face each other in the first televised debates. Viewed today, as they can be with the click of a mouse, the 1960 debates between Richard Nixon and John F. Kennedy are remarkably substantive. The candidates conducted themselves with more grace than is customary today; the questions from the moderators were serious and the answers more informative. Even then, the two campaigns played them for partisan advantage. Nixon's camp wanted no crowd shots. Kennedy insisted on newsmen as moderators.

Over the years, debates have become a staple of presidential campaigning, even as they have declined in quality and seriousness. Today, gaffes and zingers are considered "great debate" moments: Gerald Ford's 1976 head-scratcher, "There is no Soviet domination of Eastern Europe." Ronald Reagan cocking his head at Jimmy Carter and saying, "There you go again." And the famous insult Senator Lloyd Bentsen hurled at Senator Dan Quayle in their 1988 debate: "I served with Jack Kennedy. I knew Jack Kennedy. Jack Kennedy was a friend of mine. Senator, you're no Jack Kennedy."

In fairness to Dan Quayle, few men were John F. Kennedy's equal. But when we consider that Stephen Douglas and Abraham Lincoln held seven great debates—without a moderator—each lasting three hours while running for a single seat in the U.S. Senate, it's clear how far we have to go in restoring meaningful debates in American politics. Ben

Cardin was no John Kennedy, either, and he certainly wasn't Lincoln. But he should have been forced to publicly defend his record.

Duopoly Control

While there is nearly no oversight of congressional debates, presidential debates are governed by the Commission on Presidential Debates.

The CPD was established in 1987 to ensure that general election debates among the leading candidates for president and vice president are a permanent part of the electoral process. CPD describes itself as "nonpartisan," but in reality its impulses are all *bipartisan*, and it has consistently prevented third-party or independent candidates from being included in debates. Even some partisan leaders realize how wrong this is.

"The very concept of an elite commission deciding for the American people who deserves to be heard is profoundly wrong," Republican Newt Gingrich has said.[10] Liberal activist Arianna Huffington was more colorful. "Why not skip the polling," she wrote in 2000, "and just hire armed guards to gun down any threat to the two-party domination of the debates?"[11]

As a 501(c)(3) nonprofit organization, CPD can accept money from any person or corporation without having to disclose its donors. The public has no say in its leadership. And, as a non-government agency, the commission is not subject to Freedom of Information requests, meaning the commissioners and staff can keep their machinations secret.

Through the CPD, the Democrat and Republican Parties have limited the number of debates, avoided challenging formats, and excluded threatening independent and third-party candidates. Before the CPD took control prior to the 1988 election, presidential debates were sponsored by the League of Women Voters, which remains an important advocate for fair and valuable election debates.

"The League of Women Voters is withdrawing its sponsorship of the presidential debate scheduled for mid-October because the demands of the two campaign organizations would perpetrate a fraud on the American voter," League President Nancy M. Neuman said at the time. "It has become clear to us that the candidates' organizations aim to add debates to their list of campaign-trail charades devoid of substance, spontaneity and honest answers to tough questions."[12]

In the 1980 presidential race—a three-way contest between incumbent Democrat Jimmy Carter, Republican nominee Ronald Reagan, and independent John Anderson—the League of Women Voters established a baseline of 15 percent in the polls. When John Anderson met the threshold, the league invited him to join Carter and Reagan in Baltimore for the first scheduled debate. Believing that Anderson, a moderate, would take more net votes from them, Carter's camp decided to keep the president off the stage. This backfired: the president looked weak for ducking the debate, which went on without him. Moreover, his handicapping was wrong anyway: Anderson, who'd been a Republican congressman from Reagan's home state of Illinois, probably took more votes from the GOP nominee. Nonetheless, this example illustrates a mind-set that remains embedded in incumbents of both parties. It's as if they think the two-party system is a law of nature—with scarcely a thought given to the right of American voters to see and hear all the candidates.

Perhaps the most blatant example of the stranglehold the duopoly exerts through the CPD occurred in 1996, when Ross Perot was excluded from the presidential debates. Four years earlier, as an independent candidate for president, Perot had captured 19 percent of the vote after strong performances at the debates. In 1996, Perot was back, this time running as the standard-bearer of the Reform Party, which he helped create. Believing that Perot's presence had helped elect Bill Clinton in 1992, Republican nominee Bob Dole wanted to exclude Perot from the debates. Clinton's team ultimately agreed, but only in exchange for control over the format. George Stephanopoulos, senior advisor to President Clinton, explained that the Dole campaign "didn't have leverage going into negotiations. They were behind. They needed to make sure Perot wasn't in. As long as we would agree to Perot not being in it, we could get everything else we wanted going in. We got our time frame, we got our length, we got our moderator."[13]

Comfortably ahead in the polls, Clinton desired the smallest possible audience for the debates. One debate was canceled, and the remaining two were scheduled opposite the Major League Baseball playoffs. Clinton's team also insisted on a format that prohibited follow-up questions. Such behavior is typical for incumbents, who usually believe they have more to lose than gain by open and fair debates. The CPD went along for the ride.[14] Jesse Jackson, who ran for president in 1984 and 1988, called the commission "fundamentally undemocratic." Referring to Perot's exclusion, he added, "If this group can arbitrarily rule that a billionaire who gets 20 million votes and who qualifies for $30 million in election funds can't participate, then God help the rest of us."[15]

Even the *New York Times*, which is not exactly anti-establishment, was appalled. "The commission proved itself to be a tool of the two dominant parties rather than guardian of the public interest," the paper editorialized as Perot tried to get into the debates. "This commission has no legal standing to monopolize debates, and it is time for some more fair-minded group to get into the business of sponsoring these important events."[16]

Smarting from such criticism, the CPD established objective, quantitative criteria for debate qualification. A candidate would be included only if he or she met a 15 percent threshold in five separate public opinion polls. But for any third-party or independent candidate, 15 percent is an enormous hurdle. In today's modern elections, getting to 15 percent requires an expenditure of at least $266 million, according to veteran campaign consultant Douglas Schoen.* That's what it takes to build an independent candidate's name recognition and support to the point at which he or she would be invited to the presidential debates.

Over the next few elections, the CPD continued its blatantly duopolistic behavior. In 2000, Ralph Nader, who had been invited by Fox News to attend the debate, was escorted off the property under threat of arrest by police at the direction of the CPD.[17] In 2012, when Green Party presidential candidate Jill Stein and her running mate, Cheri Honkala, attempted to enter the debate hall at Hofstra University, they were held for eight hours, handcuffed to chairs. The Stein-Honkala ticket was on the ballots of 85 percent of American voters.[18]

"This is a particularly stringent test since it only takes 5 percent of the vote to qualify for public financing," Arianna Huffington noted in her 2000 column. "And it all but ensures that the Democratic and Republican nominees won't have to share the national stage with any pesky interlopers."

Even in 2016, when the two major party candidates, Donald Trump and Hillary Clinton, combined for record negative favorability ratings, the CPD denied debate access to the viable third-party candidates. In late August, a USA Today/Suffolk University poll positioned Libertarian candidate Gary Johnson at 9 percent and Jill Stein at 4 percent. The same poll found that 76 percent of Americans thought the two should

---

* Although Doug Schoen worked as a pollster and media consultant on Bill Clinton's 1996 reelection campaign, he grew disillusioned with partisan politics, and is the author of *Declaring Independence: The Beginning of the End of the Two-Party System* (2008).

be included in the debates.[19] Yet Johnson and Stein were both excluded.

The horse race nature of most political coverage compounds the injustice being done to both the candidates and voters. The absence on the debate stage of these independent and third-party candidates is used by the media as an excuse not to cover their campaigns—a perfect example of circular logic.

Since the CPD set the 15 percent barrier, no independent or third-party candidate has qualified for a presidential debate, despite the public's strong appetite for an alternative to the two major parties. To put the 15 percent figure in perspective, consider the threshold set in early 2019 by the Democratic Party for its primary debates: 1 percent.* Any candidate who polled at 1 percent or above in three polls was invited to their early debates for the 2020 presidential nomination. At the same time, it was announcing the 1 percent threshold, the Democratic Party scheduled twelve primary season debates: six in 2019 and six in 2020. Party leaders boasted that they were giving the voters as much exposure to their candidates as possible. It becomes a completely different story once they are competing outside their party. No Democrat said a word when Senator Cardin ducked a second debate in 2018.

The same exclusionary tactics are employed in the nation's governors' races. In the 2018 Arizona gubernatorial race, Green Party candidate Angel Torres was included in the September 24 Arizona PBS debate but excluded from the September 25 Arizona Public Media debate. In order to qualify for the second debate, a polling threshold was set at 7 percent, but in a catch-22 that should have embarrassed Republicans and Democrats alike, not all of the public opinion polls leading up to the debate even listed Torres's name in their surveys. This deceptive

---

*   In addition to the polling threshold, the Democratic Party set a fundraising threshold of sixty-five thousand donors for a candidate to be included in the 2019 primary debates.

ploy was used to bar Green Party candidates all over the country from sharing the debate stage with Republicans and Democrats.[20]

When given an actual choice—and by that, I mean when independents or third-party candidates are allowed to showcase their vision alongside the two major parties—Americans occasionally reveal an autonomous streak. The classic example, cherished by reformers everywhere, was Jesse Ventura's 1998 gubernatorial campaign in Minnesota. Running as a Reform Party candidate, Ventura was polling at 10 percent only six weeks before the election. But three debates later, despite not having aired any commercials, he doubled his support. On Election Day, after participating in eight debates, Ventura became the thirty-eighth governor of Minnesota.

"I was allowed to debate," he explained simply afterward. "I proved that you could go from 10 percent to 37 percent and win if you're allowed to debate. Rest assured these two parties don't want to ever see that happen again."[21]

Ventura was included because control did not rest with the two parties. The Minnesota chapter of the League of Women Voters and Minnesota Public Radio had alternated sponsorship of the eight gubernatorial debates, and they insisted that Ventura be allowed to participate.

Creating Educational and Fair Debates

A small band of committed patriots are working to fix our system of debates, focused mainly on presidential debates.

Peter Ackerman and his nonprofit, Level the Playing Field, have invested a great deal of money suing the Federal Election Commission, which is supposed to ensure that the CPD abides by federal regulations and laws. The plaintiff argues that the CPD's behavior is a violation of federal election laws that require it to remain nonpartisan and objective when determining who may participate in the presidential debates.

Suing the federal government is expensive and painstaking—and rarely successful. This case underscores that truism. In February 2017, Ackerman and his legal team were initially successful, when U.S. District Court judge Tanya Chutkan ruled that the FEC had "acted arbitrarily and capriciously and contrary to law."[22] On March 31, 2019, however, the FEC was granted a summary judgment dismissing the challenge to the commission's practices.

Another group trying to upset the existing system is OpenDebates. org. Its founder and CEO is George Farah, author of *No Debate: How the Republican and Democratic Parties Secretly Control the Presidential Debates*, a book hailed by conservative and liberal activists alike. In it, he blasts the commission as a "debate cartel" with a stifling effect on presidential elections.

Since 2012, a nonprofit called Open the Debates (a slightly different organizational name than Open Debates) has also been challenging duopoly control of presidential and statewide debates. Eli Beckerman, its founder, believes in the importance of a well-informed electorate that deserves to learn about more than just two choices on their ballot.[23] Beckerman favors ballot access as the sole criterion for inclusion in debates. I would accept some additional conditions, including a reasonable minimum poll threshold (something around 2 percent, for instance, not 15 percent), provided it's applied consistently to all candidates.

Item 2 of the Contract to Unite America seeks to replace the Commission on Presidential Debates with a new Federal Debate Commission (FDC), a truly nonpartisan entity. Remember that more Americans identify as independent than either Democrat or Republican, yet the current CPD includes no representatives for this largest bloc of American voters.

Under the existing structure, only presidential and vice-presidential debates are controlled by the CPD, while congressional debates have no oversight, other than a few guidelines from the Federal Election Commission. The new debate commission would oversee election debates for president, vice president, and the U.S. Senate and House of Representatives. It would arrange multiple debates for each election, schedule the debates at times when the public is likely to watch them, and utilize debate formats that delve into actual issues. A well-run FDC could solicit voter participation, including via social media, to determine the topics of greatest interest to the public.

The FDC would administer debates with the explicit goal of educating the public. These verbal contests have become one of the only objective ways for voters to better understand the challenges confronting our nation and the solutions proposed by potential lawmakers. Because of the documented deterioration of civics education in U.S. schools (which I'll address in chapter 10), well-watched and substantive debates have never been more important to the process of effective self-government.

Currently our debates are orchestrated to create conflict rather than to educate the public. "I saw it again, while watching the (2019) Democratic debate," wrote Amanda Ripley, an Emerson Collective senior fellow, in a guest column for the *Washington Post*. "First came the self-serious moderators, trolling for conflict. Next came the candidates, powdered and prepped."

Daring to imagine debates that would educate and enlighten rather than polarize and inflame, she went on to pose a series of bracing questions. "What would it look like if we redesigned this ritual for this polarized moment? If we accept that politicians and the media are deeply distrusted, what then?"

"One way to get people to trust you is to trust them first. In other words, journalists should ask voters what they want to know about candidates, and then deliver."

The FDC would also ensure that debates are conducted in a fair and transparent manner. The commission would act as the official "sponsor" of debates, which would no longer require sponsorship by a media partner. To determine which candidates are invited, clear minimum standards would be set, and those standards would reflect voters' growing appetite for candidates from outside the two major parties. The commission would set the number, timing, and format of debates. If a candidate refuses to show up for scheduled debates, the FDC would inform the public. Incumbents could no longer insist on unfair conditions to participate in debates or avoid them with impunity.

Self-government shouldn't come down to rivalries akin to the ones between sports franchises, just as elected officials shouldn't hide behind a football game to avoid being seen on television by voters. I didn't realize until it was too late that Ben Cardin's camp had snookered both me and the Republican challenger into debating during a Baltimore Ravens division game. Making the best of it, I quipped at one point, "The Steelers and Ravens are nicer to each other than the people in the United States Senate."

That line was quoted in the press the next day, one of the few times I was able to break through the de facto media boycott. But political debates are no joke. They are a serious part of the democratic process and have been since this country's founding. They shouldn't be treated like pawns in a game rigged by two rival franchises. They should be open, fair, educational, and—above all—accessible.

Contract Item 3

TERM LIMITS CONSTITUTIONAL AMENDMENT:

Members of the U.S. House of Representatives will be limited to three terms of two years. Members of the U.S. Senate will be limited to two terms of six years.

Sometimes Public Service
Means Letting Go

We, the American people, have a serious problem. We have 535 employees who have a profound impact on our daily lives and who are failing miserably at their jobs. Our problem is the members of the United States Congress.

They've had their performance reviews, and it didn't go well for them. In survey after survey, their collective approval rate hovers around 20 percent,[1] sometimes even lower. They get failing grades in all key areas: resolving immigration, investing in infrastructure, solidifying Social Security, improving our education system, lowering healthcare costs, reducing gun violence, preparing our workforce for the future, and controlling the growth of our debt. Straight Fs.

Fifty years ago, 75 percent of us trusted our government to do the right thing "most of the time." Today it's only 14 percent.[2]

It's pretty clear that we need to replace most of this group. We are employing the same people doing the same things but are expecting different results. As the old saying goes, this is the definition of insanity. And yet congressional retention is nearly guaranteed.[3] In 2016, the year Donald Trump rode a historic wave of anti-Washington sentiment to the White House, reelection rates for incumbents were 93 percent in the U.S. Senate and 97 percent in the U.S. House.[4] In an ideal world, elections would serve as performance reviews, with poorly performing representatives losing their seats. Unfortunately, that's not how our system works.

Americans are wise to the reasons why incumbents almost never lose. A 2015 Rasmussen poll found that 63 percent of people believe that election rules unfairly benefit incumbents.[5] Most of Congress runs in gerrymandered districts with closed primaries and have their campaigns funded by special interests who stand to benefit from their election and political parties that provide support if they toe the party line. It's nearly impossible to replace them.

According to a 2019 report by William T. Egar of the Congressional Research Service, in the past hundred years, the average tenure in the House and Senate has doubled.[6] "Career politician" should be an oxymoron. Instead, it's become more the rule than the exception. Our nation's founders envisioned a government by the people—a republic in which officeholders were farmers, teachers, lawyers, and civic leaders who came to Washington for a few years and then returned home to their professions. We have strayed too far from that vision.

Figure 1. Average Years of Prior Service in Chamber, Senators and Representatives
1st through 116th Congresses

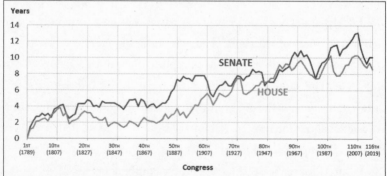

Lifetime service does not work in the private sector, and it does not work in the volunteer world. So why would it work in government?

In my businesses, when something wasn't going well, we wouldn't just pretend there was no problem. With customers to satisfy and a payroll to make, we would try different approaches: adding resources, changing strategies, and sometimes replacing personnel. New talent often brought fresh ideas and added energy. I remember a new board member who inspired an innovative way to grow our business, a new investment partner who thought creatively about our investment process, and our first chief operating officer who streamlined operations.

In my volunteer work, I also witnessed the benefit of new faces. In the past two decades, I have served on the boards of the Capital Area Foodbank, the Montgomery County Community Foundation, Interfaith Works, and the Greater Washington Community Foundation. Each of these boards consists of community servants committed to important causes. Yet, through my experiences, I came to see a profound difference in effectiveness between nonprofit boards with term limits and those without. At the Montgomery County Community Foundation, board service is limited to six years. During my time on the board, including two years as chairman, I always found the group energetic and creative.

By contrast, I was on another nonprofit board with no term limits. Some board members had served over twenty years, and the organization had grown complacent. At a recent gathering, I learned about the same "new" services that had been discussed fifteen years earlier. The belief in the benefit of new blood is widespread. Seventy-two percent of nonprofits now have limits on the number of consecutive terms board members can serve.[7]

Service to community has been a constant in my adult life, a value ingrained deeply in me as a boy. When I was twelve, I visited my father's office and noticed a framed paper on the wall with "Maimonides's Eight Levels of Tzedakah." *Tzedakah*, I knew, is the Hebrew word for charity. On the paper, the lowest level of charity was described as a situation where the donor is pained by the act of giving. The next level is when the recipient of the largesse must ask for help, but the gift is given willingly. From there, the level rises based largely on the selflessness of the donor. At the highest levels, neither the donor nor the recipient knows the other's identity.

That type of service is what I have strived to include in my own life. One of Jen's and my favorite nonprofits is called Interfaith Works. Jen, my kids, and I have volunteered periodically at their clothing distribution center. Formed as a coalition of over two hundred churches, mosques, and synagogues that came together to help those in need in Montgomery County, Interfaith Works represents service at its best: citizens of different backgrounds coming together to help other Americans. It's an organization Congress should emulate—both in its spirit of ecumenism and its belief that fresh faces bring needed dynamism.

The Parallels with Politics

Let's start by looking at the career paths of the Senate leadership. Minority Leader Chuck Schumer was first elected to the New York State Assembly in 1974 after he graduated from Harvard Law School. In 1980, he won a seat in the U.S. House of Representatives and then was reelected eight times until he left to run for the Senate in 1998. Schumer, who will turn seventy in 2020, has been in the Senate ever since.[8]

Seventy-seven-year-old Senate majority leader Mitch McConnell began running for office in high school, where he was student council president, and never really stopped. McConnell is blamed for much of the dysfunction in the Senate. In 2010, in an on-the-record interview, he said, "The single most important thing we want to achieve is for President Obama to be a one-term president."[9]

Although McConnell failed in that goal, he elevated gridlock to an actual governing strategy and helped Republicans recapture the Senate in 2010. McConnell's intransigence never waned. After the death of Supreme Court justice Antonin Scalia, he announced that the Senate would not hold hearings to consider Obama's nominee, Judge Merrick Garland, even though it meant the high court would have only eight justices for more than a year. McConnell should be at least a little sheepish about this unprecedented gambit. He's not. "One of my proudest moments," he said in a speech back home in Kentucky, "was when I looked Barack Obama in the eye and said, 'Mr. President, you will not fill the Supreme Court vacancy.'"[10]

Does having seasoned veterans like Schumer and McConnell foster a spirit of compromise on Capitol Hill? Does it help the Senate that the two have served together for decades? In a word, no. Instead, familiarity has bred contempt. The Senate's leaders don't socialize together, which was once common in Washington. They don't even spend time searching for common ground on legislation. Their priorities are getting their party to fifty-one seats in the Senate and ensuring their own reelections—not necessarily in that order.

Not to harp unduly on Ben Cardin, but he, too, first ran for office as a law school student. He ran for a seat in the state legislature that was being kept warm for him by his uncle. In his official biography, Cardin boasts of being the youngest Speaker in the history of the Maryland House of Delegates. He also expresses pride in never having lost a campaign. First elected to the state legislature in 1966, Cardin has spent his entire career in government. At the end of his current U.S. Senate term, he will have served *fifty-eight* years in office. He'll be eighty-one and has never held any job outside of politics. That's not really something to brag about.

This is par for the course among Democrats in my state. Octogenarian Steny Hoyer, the House majority leader, also first ran for a seat in the state legislature while in law school. That was in 1966. By then, Hoyer had already interned for a U.S. senator from Maryland named Daniel Brewster. Also on that staff was a Baltimore political legacy named Nancy Patricia D'Alesandro.[11] You know her as Nancy Pelosi, the Speaker of the House who has now been in Congress for over thirty years.

We have created a permanent political class, in which politicians and their staffs become the entrenched state. The longer they are in office, the more removed they become from the needs of their constituents, and the more attached they become to the power of their office. Their initial idealistic goals are often replaced by an endless struggle to retain and increase political power.

A Proud Provenance

America's Founding Fathers did not intentionally create a government dominated by career politicians. Those who foresaw the possibility warned against it. While the Constitution was being ratified by the states in 1789, Richard Henry Lee called the lack of term limits a dangerous "defect," predicting that their absence was "most highly and dangerously oligarchic."[12] Thomas Jefferson and George Mason advised limits on reelection to the Senate—and the presidency. "Nothing," George Mason inveighed, "is so essential to the preservation of a Republican government as a periodic rotation."[13]

Although they were included in the Articles of Confederation, term limits did not make it into the Constitution. But George Washington set an important precedent by stepping down as president after two terms in office. Presidents Jefferson, Madison, Monroe, and Jackson followed suit, meaning that the United States effectively had de facto presidential term limits for almost 150 years. Franklin Roosevelt's decision to run for a third term prompted passage of the Twenty-Second Amendment, which formalized the precedent set by Washington.

Congress may have sent the Twenty-Second Amendment to the states for ratification, but it wasn't a standard they applied to themselves. The "Era of Incumbency," as it has been called, was upon us, and the average term in Congress just kept getting longer.

When arriving in Washington, freshmen members of Congress were treated to the famous dictum of powerful House Speaker Sam Rayburn. To "get along" in the capital, they were told, a freshman should "go along"—meaning don't rock the boat.[14] Periodically, reformers such as the "Watergate babies" of 1974 would defy their elders or challenge the seniority system and other entrenched customs.[15] But once elected, many showed that incumbency is a highly addictive drug.

Impetus for change would come from the states, those "laboratories of democracy," in Louis Brandeis's evocative phrase. Regarding term limits, the mutiny began in Oklahoma. The rationale was explained succinctly by Cleta Mitchell, who had been an optimistic young Democrat when she won a seat in Oklahoma's legislature. "When I was first elected in 1976, I wanted to rock the boat," she recalled later. "I often told my colleagues that they should try something new. They would respond by rolling their eyes and saying, 'It's always been done this way.' Then, one day I found myself saying the same things they had. I knew it was time for me to go."[16]

By 1990, Mitchell had aligned herself with the grassroots movement that would help lawmakers know when it was "time to go." That September, Oklahomans passed a statewide referendum limiting terms for state legislators. Two months later, also through the referendum process, voters in Colorado upped the ante, making term limits a truly national issue. Coloradans limited their representatives in the U.S. House to three consecutive terms and to only two consecutive terms in the U.S. Senate.

Then, in a step that raised the stakes even further, California weighed in. Voters in the Golden State passed a referendum limiting state legislators in the California Assembly to three two-year terms and members of the California State Senate to two four-year terms. Governors were limited to two terms, plus a lifetime ban on any office once a lawmaker had reached the limit.

Outspent by more than 30–1 and opposed by leaders in both parties, the California referendum passed with 52 percent of the vote. The result sent shock waves through the political establishment. Term limits, it became clear, were not a partisan issue. Polling showed that California voters were disgusted with political bosses in both parties, and election results showed support across the ideological spectrum.

This had long been the case. Term limits were embraced by iconic American presidents ranging from Thomas Jefferson and Abraham Lincoln to John F. Kennedy. Dwight Eisenhower, who was president when the Twenty-Second Amendment passed, thought term limits should extend to Congress.[17] Harry Truman, who had served in the Senate before he was president, agreed. Truman proposed twelve-year limits on Congress but didn't get any support from his former Hill colleagues.

"Twelve years of Washington is enough for any man," Truman wrote in a White House memo expressing support for term limits. "We'd help to cure senility and seniority—both terrible legislative diseases."[18]

Term limits critics invariably insist that such restrictions limit voters' choices. To that complaint, commentator John Fund wrote in 1990 as the movement was gaining steam: "That implies we now have a choice at the ballot box."[19]

Fund cited a Common Cause report showing that as of September 30—just five weeks before that year's general election—of the 405 incumbent House members seeking reelection, seventy-eight lacked a major party opponent, and another 218 faced token opposition from candidates who'd raised less than $25,000. Another eighty-six challengers had raised half as much as the incumbent. The result, according to the Common Cause analysis, was that only twenty-three House races were remotely competitive.[20] This proved optimistic: when the votes were counted that November, only fifteen incumbents lost. Three of them faced ethics allegations.*

As a remedy to this problem, a group was formed, Americans to Limit Congressional Terms. Its thirty-five-member advisory board included eight Democrats. Several prominent liberal political commentators associated themselves with the idea too. Acknowledging that term limits would also weed out some of the best lawmakers, *New Republic* editor Hendrik Hertzberg backed it anyway. "This would be a real cost," he wrote. "But it would be a cost worth paying to be rid of the much larger number of time-servers who have learned nothing from longevity in office except cynicism, complacency, and a sense of diminished responsibility."[21]

Added *Boston Globe* columnist Ellen Goodman: "Risk-taking may come most easily with those who are willing, if necessary, to leave. If that is true, we have to learn once again that ideal public service is, by definition, temporary."[22]

---

* A fourth incumbent lost by fifty-four votes, and a fifth, Representative Peter Plympton Smith, lost to Bernie Sanders, who is still in Washington nearly three decades later.

Finally, the California vote raised the obvious implication, one Coloradans had already introduced to the national conversation: if we can enact term limits in our state capitals, why not impose the same standards on the men and women we send to Washington? A prairie fire had been ignited, and by 1992, it raged across the country.

That year, as Americans elected a new president, voters in fourteen states also set limits on congressional terms. The establishment was caught by surprise. Third-party candidate Ross Perot had pushed for term limits, but Washington elites had dismissed the issue as unimportant. The 1992 election returns showed that Perot was more aligned with the public mood than the nominees of the two major parties. Term limits, noted political analyst Dan Greenberg, received more votes than Bill Clinton in those states where they were on the ballot.[23]

Two years later, another nine states enacted laws limiting the terms of their congressional representatives. The concept consistently polled above 60 percent. At the ballot box, it was even stronger. By summer of 1994, the vote in the fifteen states that had already term-limited their congressional delegations had averaged 66 percent in favor. That year, Newt Gingrich included term limits as one of the items in the Republican Party's "Contract with America."*

But the empire was about to strike back.

In a series of lawsuits, the Democratic Party sought to get the federal courts to rule term limits unconstitutional. The case that made it to the Supreme Court, *U.S. Term Limits Inc. v. Thornton*, came from Arkansas, brought by a plaintiff named Bobbie Hill. A member of the League of Women Voters, she was a political supporter of a Democratic legislator named John Dawson, who'd served seven terms in the

---

* Term limit is the only item shared by my "Contract to Unite America" and the GOP's 1994 "Contract with America," which was a campaign strategy, albeit an effective one.

Arkansas legislature—and wanted more. Another term-limited Democrat, congressman Ray Thornton, joined the lawsuit, as did the Democratic Party of Arkansas, the ACLU, and the Clinton administration, which was headed by yet another Arkansas Democrat. This meant that, although Arkansans had voted on an overwhelming and bipartisan basis to amend their state's constitution, the case took on a partisan taint—with predictable results.[24]

In a 5–4 decision, the U.S. Supreme Court backed the establishment. The court's four conservatives voted to uphold the decision of Arkansas's voters, while the four liberal justices, joined by swing vote Anthony Kennedy, ruled that state governments cannot impose limits on candidates for federal office. Only the U.S. Constitution can do that, the court's slim majority concluded. "The right to choose representatives belongs not to the States, but to the people," wrote Justice John Paul Stevens.[25] Critics found this reasoning tortured: it was "the people" in the term limits states who had voted—and done so overwhelmingly—to set reasonable limits on the length of terms of their representatives. Depriving voters of that authority didn't empower the people. It empowered Washington insiders.

Although the Supreme Court's 1995 *Thornton* decision was denounced by Republican Party leaders, two months earlier, Gingrich as the new House Speaker, couldn't get a proposed constitutional amendment through his chamber. Although thirty-eight Democrats supported it, forty Republicans balked at supporting term limits, and the measure went down to defeat.

A Pivot Point?

I believe a new opportunity is here. In the generation since this popular grassroots movement was killed by the establishment and the Supreme Court, the costs of permanent incumbency have become even more apparent. Government shutdowns are more frequent, the federal budget process more dysfunctional, the partisan leaders more ideologically extreme, relations on Capitol Hill even more toxic, and the stranglehold of special interests even tighter. Yet, even as public confidence in Congress has plummeted, the power of incumbency remains.

Breaking that power might unlock the congressional logjams that disgust so many Americans. With more open seats, new candidates from different backgrounds and perspectives would run. Some of them would win, bringing with them innovative ideas and advisers brimming with creativity and idealism. Bending the political establishment to the will of the people on term limits would move us back toward the "citizen legislature" envisioned at our country's founding. The best people should represent us. They don't now.

Increased turnover in Washington hopefully would lead to new relationships. At one campaign event, someone asked me, "What is the very first thing you would do in the Senate?" I replied that my home is only thirty minutes from the Capitol, and I would invite senators over for dinner in groups of four: two Democrats and two Republicans. I would form personal relationships on both sides of the aisle and help them connect with each other. Mitch McConnell and Chuck Schumer have had their chance. They have chosen not to cooperate, the will of the people be damned.

Defenders of the status quo regurgitate the tired tropes of the 1990s: that term limits empower lobbyists and professional congressional staff members because they would have more sway with new members than with veterans who know the ropes. I've never bought that argument, and neither do the voters. Lobbyists themselves do not buy the argument. If they did, millions of dollars in special interest money wouldn't be funneled into campaigns against term limits. Lobbyists oppose term limits for another, more self-interested reason: they know they benefit from long term relationships with incumbent lawmakers.

With term limits in place, Congress would have more time to do real work. In the current environment, members are constantly worried about the next election. They are posturing and positioning, rather than governing. They spend half their time raising money. Under my proposal, at any given moment, almost half the Senate would be in their second term and could cease the now-endless money-raising activities.

Term limits would also bring constructive change to our government budgeting. According to Florida State University economists Randall G. Holcombe and Robert J. Gmeiner, the rate of growth in state spending was 16 percent to 46 percent lower in states with term limits for legislators.[26] Doug Bandow, a senior fellow at the Cato Institute, believes the impact could be even greater at the federal level.

"Members consistently vote for more spending the longer they stay in Congress. Once-radical critics of the federal government essentially 'go native' after serving a few terms in the nation's capital," Bandow wrote.[27] Neither party's leadership has much incentive to make tough budgetary decisions. For any politician seeking reelection, which includes almost all members of Congress, it is politically expedient to appease voters and special interests with excessive spending.

Americans Haven't Wavered

The American public overwhelmingly agrees that we need term limits. In 2018, McLaughlin & Associates conducted a poll asking, "Do you approve or disapprove of a Constitutional Amendment that will place term limits on members of Congress?" The answers were not ambiguous: 82 percent of Americans approved, including 89 percent of Republicans and 76 percent of Democrats. Only 9 percent of the survey's respondents disapproved.[28] Perhaps more telling was that 52 percent strongly approved, with only 3 percent strongly disapproving. Very few reforms enjoy this level of support.

On the campaign trail, when the topic of term limits came up, I found that nearly everyone supported the concept. Surprisingly, several voters brought up term limits as their top priority, ahead of hot-button election issues like healthcare, abortion, taxes, or impeachment.

When put to the ballot, term limits almost always win. In 2016, there were forty ballot initiatives around the country imposing term limits. All forty passed, including ballot initiatives in California, Texas, and New York. Since the 1990s, in almost every state where citizens have the power of the initiative, we have seen the adoption of term limits for state legislators. The American public has been clear about its support. It often feels that the only people not in favor of congressional term limits are the members themselves.

The concept of term limits has returned as a hot topic in the selection of congressional party leadership. Republicans term-limit their leadership positions, but Democrats do not. A group of newer Democratic representatives, led by Colorado representative Ed Perlmutter, has pushed for term limits for the three top positions in party leadership.[29] But the senior leadership of Nancy Pelosi (age seventy-nine), Steny Hoyer (age eighty), and Jim Clyburn (age seventy-nine), who would be immediately impacted, have pushed against them. Democratic committee chairs work the same way, and the average tenure is well over twenty years. Power is hard to relinquish.[30]

Yet term limits enjoy support among the most senior leaders of both major parties. Both President Obama and President Trump have expressed support for congressional term limits. "Your country is better off if you have new blood and new ideas," Obama said in 2015.[31] As a 2016 candidate, Donald Trump concurred, and as president he tweeted that he gives "Congressional term limits…[his] full support and endorsement."

In 2018, the most widely covered Senate election of the year was the Texas race pitting incumbent senator Ted Cruz against Congressman Beto O'Rourke. In this hotly contested contest, there was one topic where the ultraconservative Cruz and the liberal grassroots sensation O'Rourke agreed. They both supported term limits.

O'Rourke introduced term limits legislation in the House in 2013. And one of the first things Cruz did after being sworn in for his new term in January 2019 was propose a constitutional amendment to enact term limits. His proposal, like mine, calls for a limit on service in the U.S. Senate to two terms of six years, and in the House of Representatives to three terms of two years. Other advocates for curbing incumbency, including Democrat Tom Steyer, have called for limiting House and Senate members to twelve years each. Although I favor the shorter maximum for House members, if that compromise is what it takes to make this happen, I would enthusiastically get behind it. Any restriction on the unlimited tenure of today's career politicians would be an improvement over what we have now.

The 1994 Supreme Court ruling means that enacting term limits demands a constitutional amendment, which requires the support of two-thirds of Congress and then ratification by three-fourths of the state legislatures. It's difficult but not a pipe dream. The Constitution has been amended twenty-seven times, including six since 1951, when the president was term limited.

A new group of reformers has been laying the groundwork for the next term limits amendment. The organization, U.S. Term Limits, has collected signatures from seventy members of Congress on a pledge in support of a constitutional amendment installing term limits of three terms in the House and two in the Senate.

U.S. Term Limits is led by its executive director, Nick Tomboulides, who in 2019 testified before a Senate Judiciary subcommittee. "I come to you with a message from the American people: we demand term limits for members of Congress," he told the committee members. "This is not a left or right issue; this is an American issue."

"Now, there was a time about 25 years ago when Congress was debating this," Tomboulides added. "Nearly every opponent of term limits up here had the same rebuttal: experience, experience, experience. 'We need experience to do this job right. If only you leave your Congress member in office for decades on end, he or she will become such a policy expert that all our problems will be solved!' In hindsight, that was one of the worst predictions ever. This system is broken. Congress has given us 22 trillion dollars in debt. The longest war in American history. A broken healthcare system. A broken immigration system. A tax code written by lobbyists. An explosion of money in politics. Worst of all, too few here have the courage to solve these problems, because the only focus is on getting re-elected."[32]

When you look at how other constitutional amendments were passed, you find that there was often activity first at the state level. Take, for example, the Seventeenth Amendment, which in 1913 created direct elections for the U.S. Senate. Until then, our senators were elected by state legislatures. From 1893 to 1902, each year in Congress, there was a proposed constitutional amendment to elect senators by popular vote. And each year it failed due to resistance in the Senate. Finally, in 1907, one state, Oregon, initiated change on its own. Nebraska soon followed. By 1912, twenty-nine states had switched to direct elections of the U.S. senators. The Seventeenth Amendment was passed one year later, validating over twenty years of work by reformers.

Such success stories encourage modern change agents to believe that meaningful, even sweeping, reform of the federal government is still possible. There is palpable momentum on term limits at the local and state levels. In fifteen states, we already have term limits for the state legislatures. Thirty-six states limit terms for their governors. Some reformers are now even calling for a limit on the length of service for Supreme Court justices. We are close to a tipping point.

Item 3 of the Contract to Unite America calls for limiting House service to three terms of two years and Senate service to two terms of six years. I'm with Barack Obama, Donald Trump, Ted Cruz, and Beto O'Rourke on this. And I'm with Harry Truman, who—even though he came from the Senate and had friends there—told his old comrades that two terms "is enough."

Contract Item 4

ELECTIONS TRANSPARENCY ACT:

For any contribution of $100 or more to any candidate, party, or political entity, the donor's identity must be disclosed publicly.

The Political Black Market

In mid-September 2018, Republican challenger Matt Rosendale edged to within two percentage points of incumbent Democrat Jon Tester in Montana's close race for a U.S. Senate seat. Two years earlier, Donald Trump had carried the state in a landslide, and Democrats nationally were worried about losing the seat and, with it, any chance of taking the Senate. Suddenly, Tester's campaign was boosted by a televised blitzkrieg attacking Rosendale. One particularly snarky thirty-second spot painted him as a greedy newcomer to Big Sky Country who didn't know a cow from a cow pie and who planned to turn his rural ranch into a housing development.[1]

"Matt Rosendale may not be a rancher," the moderator intoned, as the faux cowboy in the commercial stepped in horse manure, "but he sure is full of bull."

Other than its sheer pettiness, there was nothing unusual for our politics about this attack ad, which ended with the announcer complying with the nation's impotent campaign-financing laws by saying, with the speed of an auctioneer: "Majority Forward is responsible for the content of this advertising."

Even if viewers could make out his words, this disclosure begged the question: What is "Majority Forward"?

For starters, it doesn't seem that anyone associated with the organization lives in Big Sky Country, which is ironic considering that the ad attacked Rosendale for being a carpetbagger. While the names of most of the funders were secret, some of the fat cats and special interests later became known. They include New York private equity firm executive Michael Arougheti, California billionaire and 2020 Democratic presidential candidate Tom Steyer, and the Rhode Island-based CVS pharmacy chain. Majority Forward, it turns out, is a D.C.-based "super PAC" incorporated in June 2015 by Marc E. Elias, a top Democratic Party lawyer.

A native New Yorker who lives and works in Washington, D.C., Elias was the general counsel to Democratic presidential nominee John Kerry in 2004 and Hillary Clinton in 2016 and served the same role on Kamala Harris's 2020 presidential campaign. Elias is also the party operative who hired Fusion GPS, the snooping firm that produced the "Steele dossier" used to launch the Russia investigation against Trump.[2] Elias and his firm, Perkins Coie, represent the Democratic National Committee, as well as the party's House, Senate, and gubernatorial campaign committees, and some one hundred Democratic members of Congress. According to *The Hill* newspaper, all but three Senate Democrats in the 116th Congress are clients of Elias's firm.[3]

Suffice it to say that Majority Forward is a partisan political outfit. In the 2018 election cycle, it spent $40.25 million trying to put more Democrats in Congress. Over one-tenth of that amount, $4.2 million, was spent in Montana on behalf of Jon Tester.

But the identities of those underwriting this effort—and where they got their money and what they want from Congress in return for their investment—are largely unknown. That's right. They don't have to tell us. While super PACs must disclose the names of their donors, they can take funds from entities that are not held to the same standard, meaning that the ultimate source of vast quantities of political money is essentially laundered. It's the great loophole that makes a mockery of campaign finance laws and poisons the well of our elections.

This scourge has a self-explanatory name: it's called "dark money."

Hidden Fees

Learning about dark money reminded me of when I first discovered how the wealth management industry really works. It was December 2001, and I was president and chief operating officer of a regional insurance brokerage. We were considering acquiring a wealth management business. In doing my due diligence, I was astonished by what I found.

The field of wealth management was rife with hidden fees and obvious conflicts of interest. Most customers had no idea what they were paying. Fees were buried inside funds, annuities, loans, and other products. These fees were collected invisibly and then distributed to brokers, custodians, and fund managers, each grabbing their share of the loot. Customers rarely had a clue. Brokers churned investments and then collected commissions from clients, kickbacks from the investments, or sometimes both. None of this served the interests of customers. It just made more money for those involved. It was disgusting.

In response, I launched what became my most successful company, Highline Wealth Management. Founded upon the principles of transparency and the alignment of our interests with those of our clients, Highline was an independent investment advisory that never collected hidden fees or commissions of any type. Instead, we were paid only by our clients, and we disclosed every nickel we collected. The model worked. Customers were attracted to our straightforward approach. For the seventeen years I ran the business, we grew every single year. When we sold the successor company in May 2019, we employed one hundred people and managed $6.5 billion for several thousand families and institutions.

During my 2018 campaign, I learned a great deal about U.S. politics and about the shadowy industry behind campaigns and elections in our country. The system works just like wealth management did in 2002: much of the political spending is hidden from the public, and the incentives are designed to benefit insiders, not the people. The voting public are like the clueless customers left to deal with the cost and poor results of the broken system. I was appalled and motivated to change how things are done.

Bottomless Well

Party bosses on Capitol Hill once kept envelopes of cash—a lot of it from the energy sector—to dispense to loyal party hacks. For the most part, this kind of corruption was swept away by the reforms that followed the Watergate scandal in the mid-1970s.* But in some ways, what replaced it is worse.

Today, five main types of political contributions underwrite modern campaigns for federal office:

---

* My favorite payola story comes from September 1974, when Indiana Representative John Brademas, the Democrats' whip in the House, accepted $2,950 in cash from South Korean lobbyist Tongsun Park—while participating in a conference committee on a bill prohibiting cash donations and campaign contributions from foreign nationals. Brademas's explanation? It was still legal at the time to accept the money.

1. First, there are direct contributions from individuals to a candidate's campaign coffers. Such giving has strict limits. In my Senate race, the limits were $2,700 per person during primary season and another $2,700 for the general election, for a total of $5,400 per person for an election cycle. Every individual donor must be listed publicly, by occupation and hometown.

2. The second way is to donate to political parties, a type of fundraising that puts independent candidates at a distinct disadvantage. In 2014, Senate majority leader Harry Reid (Democrat) and Speaker of the House John Boehner (Republican) didn't see eye to eye on much, but they agreed to raise the amount wealthy donors could give to a political party.[4] It's now $1.5 million per two-year election cycle. The parties can transfer up to $49,600 to each campaign, plus spend as much as they want directly on election activities.

3. Third are "political action committees" that contribute to candidates. Such PACs can collect $5,000 per person per year (but they can't take corporate or union funds) with no cap on the total amount they can raise. There's one big caveat, however: a PAC can contribute only $5,000 to an individual candidate and $15,000 to various party committees.

4. The fourth mechanism is what the Federal Election Commission calls "super PACs." Under the law, such entities can accept unlimited contributions, including union funds and money from corporate groups and very wealthy individuals (provided they are not foreign sources). Super PACs must report all their donations and expenditures to the FEC. Although this money cannot be given directly to candidates, it can be spent to influence elections so long as the officers of the super PAC do not coordinate directly with the campaign they are supporting—a murky standard that is hard to prove and even harder to prosecute.

5. Finally, the most pernicious form of political spending is done by dark money groups set up as 501(c)(4) nonprofit "social welfare" organizations. These groups are allowed to accept unlimited contributions *without disclosing their donors.* Supposedly, political advocacy cannot be their primary purpose, although "social welfare" turns out to be an elastic term. Dark money organizations cannot contribute directly to candidates. But they are permitted to produce their own political ads and funnel unlimited amounts of money to existing super PACs, which is what happened in Montana and elsewhere in 2018.

What this means is that we, the American public, very often do not know whose money is being spent on political activities. There are some serious problems with the first four types of spending, particularly the limitless funds that can be funneled into super PACs, but any fix to our corrupt campaign finance system should start with requiring full transparency. We must stop the flow of the anonymous money corrupting our political system. If we allow the identities of the donors to remain secret, there is no way to hold anyone accountable for the nasty commercials, anonymous personal attacks, deceptive mailings, straw men candidacies, and myriad other dirty tricks that epitomize modern campaigns.

"Darkness encourages bad behavior," political reformers Wendell Potter and Nick Penniman wrote in *Nation on the Take*, a book on the corrupting influence of big money in politics.[5] These groups, they believe, generate "more extreme messages, which feed the fires of polarization."

Nick, whom I've gotten to know and admire, founded Issue One, an organization dedicated to strengthening ethics laws, reducing the influence of big money on elections, and ending Washington's "pay-to-play" culture.

Its purest form is what Nick calls "transactional political giving." Lawmakers in Washington—and most state capitals—routinely solicit vast sums of campaign money from the very lobbyists being paid to influence them. It's the equivalent of a judge asking for money from an attorney handling a case in the judge's court. The conflicts of interest are so blatant that most Americans take them for granted.

Over the years, those who have looked at this normalized system of corruption have come to the same grim conclusion. Reformers Fred Wertheimer and Ralph Nader, politicians Russ Feingold and Cecil Heftel, and campaign veterans as different in outlook as Jimmy Carter pollster Patrick Caddell and disgraced Republican super-lobbyist Jack Abramoff have used the identical phrase to describe it. That phrase is "legalized bribery." (Heftel, a former congressman from Hawaii, wrote a book with that title more than two decades ago.)

Although most jurisdictions have established ethics rules limiting or prohibiting elected officials from accepting gifts (meals, travel, and other benefits) from outside sources, including lobbyists, few states have prohibited financial donations from lobbyists. South Carolina is one of the exceptions. In the Palmetto State, registered lobbyists cannot give money to a candidate running for a public office they seek to influence. It's a good rule that has been upheld for over a decade by South Carolina's courts. Unfortunately, few others have followed the example; even if they did, lobbyists could still use dark money organizations to hide their largesse.

Congress, of course, has definitely not banned the practice of allowing lobbyists to fill the campaign coffers of politicians they find reliable. A special interest can privately pitch a member of the House or Senate on its pet issues, actually submit drafts of friendly legislation to the member's staff, and then funnel money into the members' campaigns. The fact that this is legal doesn't make it any less disgusting. It's almost worse for its very brazenness. Nick Penniman uses it as a call to action.

Is Anyone Paying Attention?

Dark money isn't entirely new; what's new is its outsized influence. In 2006, campaign spending by outside groups that didn't disclose their funding totaled $5 million nationwide. By the 2008 election cycle, it had increased twenty-fold. Since 2010, spending by these opaque groups has totaled over $1 billion.

Although the rise of dark money is often attributed to the Supreme Court's *Citizens United* ruling, the surge really started before that highly controversial case was decided in 2010. It was another 5–4 Supreme Court ruling, *FEC v. Wisconsin Right to Life*, that opened the floodgates.

In that 2007 case, the Supreme Court gutted the Bipartisan Campaign Reform Act of 2002, better known as McCain-Feingold. The court ruled, by a slender conservative majority, that special interest-backed "issue ads" could not be banned sixty days prior to an election without running afoul of the First Amendment's protections of free speech. The decision opened the way for expanding independent expenditures so long as they didn't explicitly call for the election, or defeat, of a specific candidate. The era of dark money was now fully upon us and protected by a federal judiciary that gave it constitutional cover.

Citizens United, decided in January 2010, expanded on the court's logic equating money with speech. This slippery slope essentially eliminated restrictions on political spending by corporations, labor unions, and trade associations. I'll have more to say about this jurisprudence— and why we need a constitutional amendment to counteract it—in the next chapter. But when it comes to disclosure, the Supreme Court is not the problem. The problem is Congress and the two recalcitrant agencies entrusted with enforcing existing laws: the Internal Revenue Service and the Federal Election Commission.

Let's start with the IRS.

Often portrayed as a heartless federal agency that strikes fear into taxpayers' hearts, when it comes to enforcing campaign laws, the IRS is a pussycat. In the wake of the Supreme Court decisions undermining campaign finance rules, wealthy individuals and special interest groups immediately set up new vehicles to exploit the legal loopholes. The most insidious are the dark money 501(c)(4) nonprofits, which offer only vague descriptions of their expenditures. Legally, 501(c)(4) groups must spend at least 50 percent of their funds on their "primary" purpose. But the term "primary" is not explicitly defined, and this ambiguity creates an opening for those looking to buy influence.[6] For example, money spent on attack ads is sometimes earmarked as "educational" or "membership building."

This isn't merely a loophole; it's a joke. Yet the IRS does nothing about it. The results are easy to see. After jumping to $102 million in the 2008 election, dark money spending rose again in 2012 to $309 million. It dipped downward in 2016, largely because some big Republican groups took a break after Donald Trump's nomination.

Prodded by Democratic senators, the IRS tried to address these abuses during the Obama administration. The effort was bungled. The IRS slow-walked 501(c)(4) applications, but mainly of conservative groups.[7] The agency's efforts undermined potential reform, and things have only worsened. Since 2015, despite thousands of complaints from citizens and public interest groups, the IRS has not stripped a single organization of its tax-exempt status for violating spending rules. When evaluating applications for 501(c)(4) status, the IRS is equally permissive. In 2017, for example, the IRS rejected only three out of 1,487 applications.

So what about the Federal Election Commission—what's its excuse?

Established in 1974 in the crucible of Watergate, the FEC's mandate is straightforward: "To protect the integrity of the federal campaign process by providing transparency and fairly enforcing and administering federal campaign laws." Yes, that's a tall order. But after years of being undermined by the Supreme Court and sabotaged by party bosses, the agency is a sorry mess.

The FEC consists of three Democrats and three Republicans, but as I began writing this book, two seats were vacant. In September 2019, upon the departure of Vice Chairman Matthew Petersen, the organization was down to three commissioners, which makes it barely able to function, since four votes are required to take any significant action.[8]

In the meantime, enforcement of campaign finance rules has waned. Relative to the amount of money being spent on elections, the FEC has pursued far fewer campaign finance abuse cases and has levied much lower fines for wrongdoers. For the past five years, the median amount of fines issued by the FEC annually was $825,000 (in 2018 dollars), compared to $4.6 million (adjusted for inflation) in the five years following the passage of McCain-Feingold, according to Issue One.[9] The agency's enforcement division has shrunk from fifty-nine employees to forty-one, and while the FEC has the authority to write tougher disclosure requirements, they have simply failed to do so.

When the Cat's Away, the Mice Will Play

The detrimental results of inaction by the IRS and FEC are not hard to find.

In the 2018 election, a prime battleground was the U.S. Senate race in Missouri, featuring incumbent Democratic senator Claire McCaskill and her GOP challenger, state attorney general Josh Hawley. Both parties spent a fortune trying to win it. Combined, they raised and spent over $50 million, while super PACs poured in an additional $77.5 million. That totals $127.5 million on one Senate race.

Missourians had a third choice: my friend and fellow independent Craig O'Dear. While lacking the visibility and funding of his partisan opponents (he spent only about $600,000), Craig was viewed as a potentially deciding factor. McCaskill and Hawley were neck and neck throughout the campaign, and votes for Craig could push the race one way or the other. McCaskill's backers, seeing their candidate frozen in the polls in the mid-forties, hit a solution: propping up Craig at the expense of Hawley. Shortly before election day, hundreds of thousands of direct mail pieces saturated Missouri.

Featuring both O'Dear and Hawley, the mailers targeted conservatives, and falsely positioned Craig as further to the right than the Republican nominee on issues such as gun rights. The mailers were missing the legally mandated "paid for by" disclaimer, and to this day it is not known who was responsible.[10] Craig assumes, as do most political observers, that Democrats working on McCaskill's behalf executed this plan. The dirty pool wasn't enough; McCaskill lost anyway.

But sometimes such tactics succeed. Jon Tester probably wouldn't have been around to defend his seat in 2018 except for a sneaky, eleventh-hour attack funded by Washington dark money groups. In his previous election in 2012, Tester and Representative Denny Rehberg were in a virtual dead heat until the last week of the election. Then, a strange $500,000 ad campaign flooded the airwaves encouraging Montanans to vote for Dan Cox, a Libertarian.[11] Cox had raised so little money ($3,000) and had done so little campaigning that he wasn't required to file FEC reports. These pro-Cox television ads were supplemented by $40,000 in web advertising and $146,000 for slick, full-color glossy mailers. The sponsor identified itself as "Montana Hunters and Anglers."

All the messaging was designed to siphon Republican votes away from Rehberg by calling Cox the "real conservative" in the race. In some of the ads, the seven-term GOP congressman was attacked for "voting five times to increase his own pay" and for backing legislation that would give Washington bureaucrats control of vast swaths of public lands in Montana. The accusations were untrue. Rehberg never voted to raise congressional pay, and the purpose of the land use legislation was to give U.S. Customs and Border Patrol officers access to federal lands while interdicting terrorists crossing the Canadian border.

The name of the group itself was sketchy. While Montana Hunters and Anglers was run by an actual Montanan named Land Tawney who does, in fact, hunt and fish, the group's funding was almost entirely from out of state. Tawney is no Libertarian; he's a Democratic activist who supported Barack Obama in 2012. Tawney was really a front for the super PACs and Democratic Party–oriented dark money groups that funded Montana Hunters and Anglers.

In the end, the last-minute bombardment almost certainly decided the election. Tester won by 18,000 votes out of 486,000 votes cast. The late surge toward Dan Cox gave the Libertarian 32,000 votes—or 6.6 percent—to a candidate who figured to get 1 percent. This is why reformers such as Nick Penniman call dark money "the most toxic force in politics."[12]

Over the years, enterprising investigative journalists have tried to shine a light on this odious black market, but it's nearly impossible to keep pace with the purveyors of politics' dark arts. In 2014, a *Washington Post* exposé revealed that Charles and David Koch, the conservative billionaire brothers and Republican campaign financiers, had expanded their political network "into a far-reaching operation of unrivaled complexity, built around a maze of groups that cloaks its donors, according to an analysis of new tax returns and other documents."[13]

While the *Post* article was illuminating, it was published too late for voters to factor this information into their election decisions. The 2012 election season was not a good one for Republicans, but it would have been worse if not for the Koch network. Operating under front groups with names such as American Commitment, American Future Fund, and Crossroads GPS, Koch money was used for eleventh-hour blitzkriegs in close House and Senate races. In Nevada, it helped Republican Dean Heller stave off a Democratic challenge in the country's closest Senate race; in Arizona, Koch money propelled Jeff Flake to victory in another tight race. According to the Center for Responsive Politics, the Koch network alone was responsible for more than one-fourth of all dark money reported in the 2012 election cycle.[14]

Two years later, the same network reached deep into the weeds of Iowa politics to elevate a little-known state legislator named Joni Ernst to the 2014 GOP nomination for an open Senate seat. Bruce Braley, her eventual Democratic opponent, felt the sting of negative ads financed by Koch money beginning in April.[15] Braley was accused of taking "tens of thousands of dollars from his friends in the health insurance industry" and of causing thousands of Iowans to lose their medical insurance. This mendacious ad was debunked by the fact-checking website PolitiFact.[16] For his part, Braley tried to make sure voters knew the attacks on him were fueled in part by the Koch operation. Braley also benefited from out-of-state, Democratic dark money, but it wasn't enough. When it was over, Joni Ernst was a U.S. senator.

The Solution

I'm not trying to reinvent the wheel here. Other than the Missouri example, these case studies are from reports by Issue One and media outlets ranging from the New Yorker and Politico to ProPublica, a non-profit that does important investigative journalism. New Yorker staff writer Jane Mayer was one of the first to blow the whistle on the proliferation of dark money; her interest piqued while writing a 2010 profile of Charles and David Koch. Mayer turned her piece into a 2016 book, Dark Money: The Hidden History of the Billionaires Behind the Rise of the Radical Right.

By the time Mayer's book was finished, billionaires and deep-pocketed organizations on the other side of the political spectrum had entered an arms race with their conservative opponents. Republican funders such as Sheldon Adelson, the U.S. Chamber of Commerce, and the National Rifle Association were rivaled by pro–Democratic Party billionaires George Soros, Michael Bloomberg, and Tom Steyer, as well as Planned Parenthood, EMILY's List, and the ubiquitous Majority Forward. In the 2018 elections—the most expensive midterms in U.S. history—liberal groups actually outspent conservative groups, 54 percent to 46 percent.

George Soros took things to a new level by "going granular." His money was behind groups supporting progressive lawyers competing in local prosecutors' elections around the country. In Northern Virginia, two longtime commonwealth attorneys were replaced by progressive insurgents who cooperated closely with Soros-controlled super PACs, something that wouldn't be allowed in a federal election. According to the *Washington Post*, Soros's Justice & Public Safety super PAC donated more than $1 million to progressive challengers in two Virginia counties where elections normally cost a fraction of that amount.[17]

But this grim new reality actually presents an opportunity. Now that left-leaning groups deploy as much dark money as conservative groups, each side has an incentive to come to the bargaining table. In early 2019, at a meeting on Capitol Hill, Jim Rubens, a former state senator in New Hampshire, made a persuasive case for disclosure rules and then added candidly, "We may as well support disclosure requirements. There is no longer any advantage for Republicans with this type of funding."

One bipartisan proposal introduced in Congress, the Political Accountability and Transparency Act, would require disclosing the top donors to organizations paying for advertisements and strengthen rules barring coordination between super PACs and campaigns. Another proposal, the Honest Ads Act, would hold online political communications to the same standards that now exist for advertisements on television, print, and radio. Our failure to recognize, let alone regulate, the power of social media was one of the great failings of the 2016 presidential campaign, and left the door open to Russian attempts to manipulate the U.S. electorate.

Meanwhile, several states have acted. New Jersey now requires nearly all 501(c)(4)s to disclose their donors. California recently mandated the disclosure of nonprofit donors who give $5,000 or more. Other initiatives are underway in Arizona, Idaho, and Oklahoma. National groups such as Take Back Our Republic, American Promise, the Brennan Center, and the Center for Political Accountability are pushing hard as well. All of them support transparency because they understand that it leads to better behavior. I saw this in financial services. People behave better when they know someone is watching.

What we really need is federal legislation. Item 4 of the Contract to Unite America calls on Congress to mandate full transparency for all political donations of $100 or more. The American public deserves to know whose money is bankrolling political advertisements—the true identities of the donors, not some Orwellian name like "Freedom Path." America's real path to freedom is transparent, honest campaigns.

You know who agrees with me? None other than Senator Jon Tester. Although he benefited from dark money in both 2012 and 2018, it's not a system he created—and dark money has been used *against* him as well. Tester co-sponsored legislation requiring full disclosure and has been vocal in the Senate about it.

"You've got groups with really nice-sounding names dumping millions of dollars into these campaigns that quite frankly aren't being totally honest," Tester said after being reelected. "They're not being honest with the people about who's paying for the ads, and the ads stretch the truth a long ways, let's just put it that way."

Contract Item 5

CAMPAIGN FINANCE CONSTITUTIONAL AMENDMENT:

Government may distinguish between corporations and people, and Congress and the states can apply reasonable limits on campaign spending.

Unlimited Spending and Dishonest Graft

It is no mere quirk of fate that Montana is a key battleground in the fight over the corrupting influence of corporate political money. The "Treasure State," as it was known, has been an epicenter on this issue since before any current member of Congress—or the U.S. Supreme Court—was born.

The "treasure" in that nickname referred to Montana's vast mineral resources, and at the beginning of the twentieth century, the "Copper Kings" of Butte controlled the state's politics with the most basic possible tool: they bribed lawmakers. At a time when state legislatures still picked U.S. senators, one of the Copper Kings even purchased a Senate seat. William A. Clark was his name, and the Senate initially refused to seat him. Although Clark eventually served one term in Washington, his sordid escapade helped generate support for the Seventeenth Amendment, which established direct vote of senators.[1]

The power of the Copper Kings, and their Anaconda Copper Mining Company, was not easily thwarted, however. In 1906, Miles Romney, a crusading newspaper editor and reform-minded Montana Democrat, described the stakes this way: "The greatest living issue confronting us today is whether the corporations shall control the people, or the people shall control the corporations."[2]

Montanans have made it clear where they stand. In 1912, its voters approved a ballot initiative called the Corrupt Practices Act outlawing corporate contributions in state elections, while imposing strict caps on donations by individuals. As recently as 1994, its voters tightened the limits even further: $100 was the maximum contribution to a candidate for the legislature; $400 for governor or lieutenant governor.[*] This applies to political action committees as well as individuals.

Montana's system has withstood direct legal challenges and has survived in stark contrast to the system in place for federal elections. On average, the winner of a Montana state senate race spends only $17,000 on the campaign. As then-governor Brian Schweitzer noted with pride in 2012, Montana's system has "nurtured a rare, pure form of democracy."[3]

But that form of "pure democracy" would not withstand an onslaught of federal jurisprudence that essentially removed all campaign spending limits. By now most Americans have heard of the infamous 2010 *Citizens United* case, even if they don't know its details. Democrats especially revile this ruling, but so should we all. It was the culmination of a generation of problematic Supreme Court decisions that have made it impossible to limit spending in U.S. political campaigns, including by corporations. Ever since then, it's been like the Wild West.

---

[*]   Indexed for inflation, the amounts in 2019 had risen to $180 for legislative races and $680 for a governor or lieutenant governor's race—double that if there is a primary election.

No-Limit Poker

In 2018, more than $70 million was spent in the U.S. Senate race in Montana, a state of only one million people. Indiana's Senate race burned through $113 million, a figure Florida topped by a stunning $100 million. Nevada, which has just over three million people, surpassed $108 million in 2018—$92 million of it from out of state. In 2016, another Nevada Senate race cost $122.6 million, meaning that nearly one-quarter of a billion dollars was spent over a two-year span by the two major political parties and their special interest allies trying to gain a single R or D in the U.S. Senate.

Probably the most amount ever spent *per capita* on an election in this country also came in 2016, the U.S. Senate race in the tiny state of New Hampshire. There, in a state where voters pride themselves on taking politics seriously and knowing the issues, $131.6 million was spent—$93 million from out of state—most of it on attack ads funded by super PACs or out-of-state dark money groups. To citizens active in New Hampshire's civic affairs, such spending undercuts the state's entire political culture. In the 2016 gubernatorial race, for instance, an estimated 80 percent of the $14.2 million in independent expenditures came from out-of-state special interest groups. On the left, these sources ranged from billionaires George Soros, Michael Bloomberg, and Tom Steyer to Planned Parenthood and the National Education Association—the nation's largest teachers' union. On the right, the sources included Comcast, Big Pharma, and the Koch network–backed Americans for Prosperity.

What's the harm in this? Let us count the ways.

First, in the New Hampshire example, why should wealthy non-residents be able to exert huge influence on elective offices that ought to be nobody's business unless they live there? Why, for that matter, should one American's voice be ten thousand times as influential as another's? Because they have more money?

It also creates a pay-for-play culture that corrupts the system. Allowing unlimited money to influence campaigns allows corporations, industries, and other special interests to buy influence that isn't available to less well-heeled opponents, which shouldn't be available to anyone. The pharmaceutical industry is a good case study. During the last Congress, twenty members of the House and Senate received $165,000 or more from the pharmaceutical and health sector. Thirteen were Republicans, and seven were Democrats. The top two were senators: Republican Mitch McConnell and Democrat Cory Booker. Predictably, with so many congressional leaders in its pocket, Big Pharma has benefited from public policy skewed toward its interests. Politicians supported by the industry have prevented the government from negotiating drug prices used by Medicare patients, adding billions of dollars in taxpayer costs. They have also prevented the importation of drugs that, while originally manufactured in the United States, sell for much lower prices overseas. The result? Drug spending per capita in the United States is double the average among industrialized countries.[4]

If such influence peddling resulted in the kind of "honest graft" that the Tammany Hall political machine once prided itself in, one could argue that the system works despite its unsavory appearances. But it doesn't. A 2014 study done by Princeton professor Martin Gilens and Northwestern University scholar Benjamin Page examined congressional action on 1,779 policy issues and found that "when the preferences of economic elites and the stands of organized interest groups are controlled for, the preferences of the average American appear to have only a miniscule, near-zero, statistically non-significant impact on public policy."[5]

In other words, no correlation exists between legislation and what is actually good for Americans. The correlation is with who gives money. The system of unlimited, and barely regulated, campaign donations doesn't produce anything approaching "honest" graft. It's just graft. Another description would be "legalized bribery."

Americans get this intuitively, which leads to another corrosive consequence of the current system—a jaded electorate. A 2015 Rasmussen poll found that 58 percent of Americans believe that most members of Congress will sell their votes for cash or campaign contributions.[6] Obviously, Americans who believe their congressional representatives are for sale lose trust in their own government. Also, limitless election spending fuels the incredible negativity of our campaigns, increasing the toxicity—and dysfunction—of our politics.

And though the candidates know all this themselves, there isn't any way for them to unilaterally avoid the spending race. In my own Senate bid, I hired a professional staff at a budget of $75,000-per-month, visited all twenty-three Maryland counties and the city of Baltimore, met thousands of voters, and still only reached 4 percent in the early horse race polls. We began investing our campaign reserves on thirty-second television spots, attempting to carve out support before the airwaves were saturated with political ads. Within two weeks, we doubled our support to 8 percent. Three weeks later, at the start of October, we were at 18 percent. With $500,000 spent on advertising, we had quadrupled our support.

Although I also benefited from a successful debate, the main driver was the commercials. We would go all in, gambling all our remaining campaign funds on additional advertising. Ben Cardin took notice. With six years to raise money, the power of incumbency, and an affiliation with the state's dominant political party, he had considerable resources. Cardin's $4 million dwarfed our remaining balance, and he started to spend it. Although he had raised far less than most incumbent senators, he could afford to outspend us nearly tenfold over the next two weeks. The ads were effective. We dropped in the polls, while he gained. Yes, there were other dynamics during those weeks, including the deeply partisan and controversial Senate Judiciary Committee hearings on Brett Kavanaugh's Supreme Court appointment that galvanized the bases of both parties. But the real variable was Cardin's war chest.

"There are two things that are important in politics," Ohio Senator Mark Hanna and onetime head of the Republican National Committee said in 1895. "The first is money and I can't remember what the second one is."[7]

Members of Congress understand this. Numerous studies have shown that elected officials in the House and Senate spend half their time raising money.[8] *Half their time.* This might be a conservative estimate. According to former Senate Democratic leader Tom Daschle, it's worse than that. "A typical United States Senator," Daschle said after leaving office, "spends two-thirds of the last two years of their term raising money."[9]

Lawrence Lessig, a Harvard Law School professor and passionate reformer, calls the current system "pathological, democracy-destroying corruption."[10] Lessig feels so strongly about reducing the influence of money in politics that he briefly ran for president in 2016 to draw attention to the issue. Larry thinks Congress's own conflicts of interest are so profound when it comes to campaign financing that they can no longer stand up to the big donors.[11]

So why are we saddled with such a terrible system? And how do we fix it? The path to finding answers to those questions begins on Capitol Hill and takes us beyond Washington to the state capitals—for a solution that reformers are already calling the Twenty-Eighth Amendment.

Hard Cases and Bad Law

In 1904, two years before Miles Romney threw down the gauntlet on corporate money in politics, Oliver Wendell Holmes noted while weighing an antitrust case before the Supreme Court that "hard cases make bad law." As his colleagues understood, Justice Holmes was invoking an aphorism that had been a staple of Anglo American jurisprudence since the early 1800s. Writing the dissent in a 5–4 decision, the famed jurist lamented that such cases "exercise a kind of hydraulic pressure, which makes what previously was clear seem doubtful, and before which even well-settled principles of law will bend."[12] So what happens when two "well-settled principles" are at odds?

I'm referring to free speech and fair elections. In trying to balance these two hallowed values, the U.S. Supreme Court has repeatedly, albeit by narrow margins, come down on the side of free speech. In "hard" cases going back to the mid-1970s, the high court has held that the First Amendment takes precedence over attempts by Congress and state legislatures to set rules designed to ensure fair and meaningful elections. Legal scholars critical of the majority opinions in these cases believe the court has distorted the First Amendment by conflating the free speech rights of powerful elites with the free speech rights of all Americans. The net results have been unfair and increasingly obnoxious elections—and a broken political system. Hard cases have definitely made bad law—and, over time, produced bad lawmakers.

In the previous chapter, I called on Congress, the Federal Election Commission, and the IRS to do their jobs—to bring complete transparency into the American political system. For example, if something called the Center to Protect Patients' Rights—an unknown group that pumped $137 million into campaigns from an Arizona box office address in 2012 alone—was really billionaire brothers Charles and

David Koch, then voters had a right to know about it before they went to the polls.[13] But public disclosure, while a good start, is not nearly enough. The mortal sin is that far too much money, from a small, albeit powerful, segment of American society, is spent trying to manipulate voters, influence elections, and compromise officeholders.

Recognizing sin and avoiding it are two different things, however.

The first big push to clean up modern U.S. politics came in the wake of the Watergate scandal that ended Richard Nixon's presidency. In 1968, Nixon had raised $25 million—twice as much as losing Democratic candidate Hubert Humphrey. Even when adjusted for inflation, that's only as much as a competitive Senate race costs today. Democrats were shocked at such a sum and sought to prevent anything like it from happening again. The legislation they produced, the Federal Election Campaign Act of 1970, was passed by Congress and promptly vetoed by President Nixon. In response, Congress passed a second, slightly altered version, which Nixon signed into law on February 7, 1972.

The new statute established the Federal Election Commission, set limits on contributions that candidates and their families could spend on campaigns, capped how much money could be used for political advertising, and required full disclosure of all donations.*

Calling it "a realistic and enforceable bill," Nixon pronounced himself "pleased to give [it] my approval."[14]

What he didn't mention is that Congress gave the two political parties—and the already active presidential campaigns—sixty days to comply with the law, a delay that prompted a grubby chase for high-dollar donations from wealthy contributors, some of whom would never be

---

* The legislation also strengthened long-standing prohibitions against corporations making direct contributions to political campaigns, a measure first enacted in a 1907 statute known as the Tillman Act, but lacked enforcement provisions and was, consequently, widely ignored.

identified.[15] One of those who *was* known was W. Clement Stone, a Chicago insurance tycoon who loved Nixon and vowed to spend millions on his behalf. The exact amount is unknown to this day, but among the abuses uncovered during Watergate was a briefcase stashed with $1.8 million of Clement Stone's cash. After the scandal, Congress imposed new donation limits of $2,000 per person per election cycle and strict reporting requirements. Groups could donate up to $5,000. Groups of wealthy individuals could spend up to $50,000 advocating on their own behalf.

These reforms were immediately challenged in federal court. In a 1976 decision, *Buckley v. Valeo*, the court upheld the principle that Congress could regulate such spending but tossed out the limit that candidates can personally spend on their own campaigns, which the court ruled was a violation of the First Amendment. This was the first of a spate of cases that would undermine the ability of America's elected representatives to keep corporate money, billionaires' money, and special interest money out of political campaigns.

The next test came in Michigan, where lawmakers passed a law prohibiting corporations from spending general funds "on independent expenditures to support or oppose candidates in elections for state offices." It was hardly a draconian piece of legislation: it contained a big loophole—corporations with independent accounts designed for political activity could still use those funds for such purposes. Seeing this as a slippery slope, however, the Michigan Chamber of Commerce challenged its constitutionality. The case made it to the U.S. Supreme Court, which upheld it in 1990. In a 6–3 decision written by Thurgood Marshall, the high court signaled its sympathy for laws aimed at fighting what Marshall called "a different type of corruption in the political arena: the corrosive and distorting effects" of big-dollar donors.[16]

Austin v. Michigan Chamber of Commerce was a victory for reformers. Two more were coming. The first was the Bipartisan Campaign

Reform Act of 2002, known as McCain-Feingold after its two principal sponsors, Democratic senator Russ Feingold from Wisconsin and Arizona's Republican senator, John McCain. The second was a 2003 Supreme Court decision validating it. McCain-Feingold set limits on the money corporations, unions, and wealthy individuals could donate to political parties or their affiliated organizations. A second part of the law, tailored to pass the constitutional muster set out in *Austin*, prohibited corporations or unions from using general funds for "electioneering communications" that referenced a candidate for federal office within thirty days of a primary or sixty days of a general election.

The statute was promptly challenged in federal courts by an array of special interest groups on the left (the AFL-CIO) and the right (the National Rifle Association)—as well as the California Democratic Party and the Republican National Committee. The case took its name from McCain-Feingold's main opponent in Congress, Mitch McConnell. In 2003, the Supreme Court upheld McCain-Feingold. Writing for the majority, Justice John Paul Stevens ruled that the statute's restrictions were justified by government's interest in precluding "both the actual corruption" of large financial contributions and the "appearance of corruption" that such donations implied.[17]

Yet there were warning signs that the court's certitude was crumbling. For one thing, the decision this time was 5–4, not 6–3, as it had been in *Austin* thirteen years earlier. Also, *McConnell vs. F.E.C.* was a confusing ruling—with eight separate opinions—in which all nine justices dissented in part and affirmed in part. One of the clearest voices, if not the most reform minded, belonged to Clarence Thomas, who wrote in a separate twenty-page dissent that the majority had upheld the "most significant abridgment of the freedoms of speech and association since the Civil War."[18]

It didn't seem as though this jumble of written opinions could be the last word, and it wasn't. Four years later, in a 2007 case called *F.E.C. v. Wisconsin Right to Life Inc.*, the court reversed field. McCain-Feingold sought to outlaw campaign attack ads masquerading as "issue ads." But who decides whether an issue ad is a sham campaign ad or protected political speech of utmost civic importance? McCain-Feingold left that decision up to the FEC, which meant a test case was inevitable, and it came in Russ Feingold's home state in the midst of his own 2004 reelection campaign.

Late that year, the Wisconsin Right-to-Life Committee produced political ads mentioning Feingold by name. Ostensibly, the spots urged voters to call the state's two senators and complain about Senate Democrats' filibustering against George W. Bush judicial appointments. To the FEC, the obvious purpose of the ads was to rile up prolife voters against Feingold's reelection. It was a classic case of "bad facts" making bad law. The ads did have an educational purpose and were clever as well. One opened with a wedding scene and a pastor asking, "And who gives this woman to be married to this man?" Here's the rest of the text:

> BRIDE'S FATHER. Well, as father of the bride, I certainly could. But instead, I'd like to share a few tips on how to properly install drywall. Now you put the drywall up...

> VOICE-OVER. Sometimes it's just not fair to delay an important decision. But in Washington, it's happening. A group of senators are using the filibuster delay tactic to block federal judicial nominees from a simple "yes" or "no" vote. So qualified candidates don't get a chance to serve. It's politics at work, causing gridlock and backing up some of our courts to a state of emergency. Contact Senators Feingold and Kohl and tell them to oppose the filibuster.

This was the first time the Supreme Court under Chief Justice John Roberts was weighing First Amendment concerns against campaign finance laws. The result was different. "Enough is enough," Roberts wrote in a 5–4 decision in favor of Wisconsin Right-to-Life. "Issue ads like WRTL's are by no means equivalent to contributions, and the *quid-pro-quo* corruption interest cannot justify regulating them."[19]

Ultimately, the court reversed its rulings in the *Austin* and *McConnell* cases. Writing in dissent, Justice David Souter noted the court's abandonment of its own recent precedent. He also made a broader point that would prove highly prescient.

"Neither Congress's decisions nor our own have understood the corrupting influence of money in politics as being limited to outright bribery or discrete *quid pro quo*," Souter wrote. "Campaign finance reform has instead consistently focused on the more pervasive distortion of electoral institutions by concentrated wealth, on the special access and guaranteed favor that sap the representative integrity of American government and defy public confidence in its institutions."

That erosion of public confidence in the nation's institutions—including the Supreme Court itself—would be exponentially accelerated three years later in a now-notorious case.

Citizens Divided

The 1988 presidential campaign featured Vice President George Bush against Massachusetts governor Michael Dukakis, who touted his management skills as the overseer of the "Massachusetts Miracle" (i.e., the Bay State's strong economy).

Republican opposition researchers, looking for flaws in that "miracle," came across a prison furlough program that had temporarily released violent felons, some of whom had committed crimes while on weekend passes. One of them, a convicted murderer named William Horton, went to Maryland, where he committed a brutal home inva- sion, raping a woman and nearly killing her fiancé. The Bush campaign highlighted this horror story in a thirty-second spot called "the revolving door ad," which pictured inmates going through a turnstile. Sensitive about the racial angle—Horton was black, his victims white—Bush media maven Roger Ailes obscured the racial angle by filming in a Utah prison using sepia tones.[20]

Two conservative provocateurs named Floyd Brown and David Bossie found the Ailes approach too genteel. So they formed a nonprofit, produced a low-budget ad of their own, and bought cheap air time on a late-night cable station. Their idea was to attract "free media" attention for their crude commercial featuring a menacing-looking Horton with a wild Afro. Their scheming worked, and not for the last time. They had named their nonprofit Citizens United.

Fast-forward to the 2004 presidential cycle, when Citizens United filed a complaint with the FEC about *Fahrenheit 9-11*, an unlikely block- buster by progressive filmmaker Michael Moore. Employing his familiar cinematic devices—exaggeration, snark, and key omissions—Moore's film was a polemic, not history. But polemics have always been part of politics. It's just that the 2004 campaign between Bush and John Kerry was the first presidential election since McCain-Feingold became law, and Citizens United asserted in its court filing that *Fahrenheit 9-11* was basically a paid political ad that couldn't be legally aired within sixty days of a federal election.

The claim was rejected, so Citizens United produced its own propa- ganda film, *Hillary: The Movie*, in time for the 2008 campaign. As they'd done with the Willie Horton ad, the group bought time for it on a cable station. This time, the FEC did take exception. Citizens United sued, and the ensuing litigation produced one of the most contentious and consequential Supreme Court rulings in modern history.

"When government seeks to use its full power, including criminal law, to command where a person may get his or her information or what distrusted source he or she may not hear, it uses censorship to control thought," Justice Anthony Kennedy wrote for the 5–4 majority in neutering McCain-Feingold. "This is unlawful. The First Amendment confirms the freedom to think for ourselves."[21]

To the four justices in the minority, and eventually to a majority of Americans, the defining characteristic of the *Citizens United* decision was not that it upheld free speech. It was that the decision had the perverse effect of giving U.S. corporations the same constitutional rights as citizens. In a fiery ninety-nine-page dissent, Justice Stevens made this very point. Congress, Stevens wrote, has just as much right to regulate the buying and selling of airtime as it does to curb the buying and selling votes—and that the effect is the same.

In the ensuing decade, Stevens's warnings have been validated, just as Justice Souter's have been. The deleterious effects of the Supreme Court decisions didn't take long to manifest themselves. And as another presidential election unfolds ten years after *Citizens United*, this is the environment we find ourselves in:

+ Spending in 2016 reached $6.9 billion, and 2014 and 2018 set new records for spending in a midterm election.

+ In 2012, 93 percent of super PAC funding came from 3,300 donors—in a country of 320 million people.

+ Most spending is used for negative campaigning, making sure our politics is increasingly ugly and more toxic.

- The political industrial complex now employs nearly twenty thousand people, including lobbyists, campaign consultants, paid campaign staff, and staff at partisan think tanks.

Pay-to-play government has been institutionalized. Groups such as the U.S. Chamber of Commerce, the National Rifle Association, the Pharmaceutical Research & Manufacturers of America, the American Federation of Teachers, the Service Employees International Union, and individuals such as Charles Koch, Sheldon Adelson, Tom Steyer, George Soros, and Michael Bloomberg are funneling hundreds of millions of dollars into politics in realistic hopes of influencing government policy.

The Solution

Progressives will counter that Steyer, Soros, and Bloomberg aren't paying to play; they're paying it back. I take their point. I do not believe that Mike Bloomberg is trying to buy politicians to increase his company's profitability. But think about this another way. Imagine you are an ordinary American who disagrees with the progressive policy solutions advocated by Steyer, or the conservative positions of the Kochs. Why should these men have a million times as much influence in U.S. politics as the average American?

"At a critical level, contributions that underwrite elections are leverage for enormous political influence," is how David Souter put it. "Voters know this. Hence, the second important consequence of the demand for big money to finance publicity: pervasive public cynicism."[22]

Souter's warning went unheeded by a majority of his fellow justices, however, and since his retirement, the Supreme Court has become even less responsive to the problem. To me, the bottom line is simple:

Even if the IRS cracked down on the fiction that groups formed for the sole purpose of airing party-affiliated political attack ads are really "social" organizations performing educational functions, it wouldn't be enough. Even if the FEC enforced election laws already on the books regarding the covert cooperation between super PACs and political parties, it wouldn't be enough. Even if Congress passed a new law requiring full disclosure of political donations, it wouldn't be enough. Even if all those things happened simultaneously, it wouldn't be enough. There is simply too much money in American politics, and it has warped our ability to practice self-government. What is required is a constitutional amendment that unspools *Citizens United* and the other like-minded judicial decisions.

"Without reasonable limits on money in elections, we are fast on our way to oligarchy," is how influential reformer Jeffrey D. Clements explains it. "We need a constitutional amendment because the Supreme Court has left us no choice if we want to stop corruption and put power into the hands of the people."[23]

Clements is the founder and president of American Promise, a group seeking to do just that. American Promise is but one of a dozen groups seeking relief from the tyranny of *Citizens United*, and although I applaud them all, Jeff's meticulous nonpartisanship appeals to me the most. This approach also seems to be making the most progress.

In late June 2019, New Hampshire became the twentieth state to adopt, either by legislative action or citizen referendum, a resolution encouraging Congress to pass legislation for what reformers are already calling the Twenty-Eighth Amendment. The theory behind this strategy is that if the impetus comes from the states, where any amendment would have to be ratified, the entrenched Washington duopoly will be forced to respond. Among those twenty states are "red" Wyoming, "blue"

California, and many "purple" swing states such as New Hampshire.

"Millions of Americans are coming together to work for a constitutional amendment so every American has free speech and representation in our political system," adds Jeff, whose book title succinctly sums up the fight: *Corporations Are Not People: Reclaiming Democracy from Big Money and Global Corporations.*

We've come a long way in American politics since 2011 when, on a hot August day, Mitt Romney responded to a heckler at the Iowa State Fair by saying, "Corporations are people, my friend."[24]

Although Romney was widely ridiculed for that ad-libbed remark, he wasn't even talking about campaign finance laws, let alone *Citizens United.* He was talking about tax policy. And what he was really saying was, "Hey, don't demonize corporations because if you raise taxes on them, they pass that along to real people."

I get that. I'm from the world of business myself. I owned a company. I don't want to demonize business—or the Supreme Court, for that matter. I just want to constrain the unlimited influence of corporations, billionaires, and special interests.

It's what the American people want, too, and what good-government advocates have been trying to do for more than a century.

I believe that Miles Romney, a cousin of Mitt Romney, had it exactly right back in 1906 when he advocated for limits on campaign contributions. Today, Jeff Clements and the many activists trying to undo *Citizens United* and the other "bad fact" Supreme Court cases have it right too. I'd offer one small caveat. If we pass a constitutional amendment on term limits first, the measure being proposed by American Promise would be the Twenty-Ninth Amendment to the Constitution, not the Twenty-Eighth. I had dinner with Jeff while writing this book, and he assured me with a smile that this wouldn't be a sticking point.

Contract Item 6

BALLOT ACCESS ACT:

To be included on an election ballot, all candidates will be subject to identical requirements, which cannot exceed five thousand signatures on a petition.

Let My People Run

Heading home on a southbound Amtrak train in early summer 2018, I received a disturbing phone call. I had been to Manhattan to speak at a Unite America event hosted by Scott Sipprelle and Owen Thomas, two friends and campaign supporters. The call, however, had nothing to do with the luncheon in New York or my race in Maryland. It was about a campaign in Texas.

On the line was Jonathan Jenkins, a Dallas-area technology entrepreneur, who was making an independent bid for the Senate seat held by Ted Cruz. As we mounted our parallel efforts, Jonathan and I had shared insights from the campaign trail. The last time we had spoken, he was poised to submit more than the forty-seven thousand signatures required as an independent to be included on Texas's general election ballot. To accomplish this Herculean task, Jonathan had mobilized thirty volunteers and paid more than $500,000 to a prominent petition-gathering company, a standard practice for independent campaigns.

In most states, officials from the two major parties have erected formidable barriers that third-party and independent candidates are forced to overcome before being listed on the ballot. Texas's hurdles are perhaps the toughest. In addition to having one of the highest signature requirements, the Lone Star State allows only three months to complete the task and prohibits anyone who has voted in either the Democratic or

Republican primary from signing. Moreover, in order to discourage the collection of such petitions, Texas requires those gathering signatures to read aloud a minute-long oath to each signatory requiring them to swear that they did not vote in a primary election.

Since 1905, Texas has never modernized the petition requirements to reflect the reality of present-day communications. Instead, over the decades it heightened roadblocks for any candidate who is not a member of the two dominant political parties.[1] In 1967, the Texas legislature expanded its requirement that independent candidates gather signatures from 1 percent of the state's voters to minor party candidates as well. In 1987, the state advanced its deadline for an independent presidential primary candidate to garner signatures from July to May. It also requires that an independent candidate choose a running mate before gathering signatures. In other words, independents must name their vice-presidential choice months before Republicans and Democrats do so.[2]

The results of such double standards are predictable. It's exceedingly difficult, and expensive, for independents in Texas to get their names on the ballot in statewide races.[3] One exception was in 2006 when longtime Texas Republican Carole Keeton Strayhorn and colorful Texas musician Kinky Friedman spent the huge amounts of money required to gather such signatures in their runs for governor. Strayhorn finished third in the five-person field headlined by incumbent Republican governor Rick Perry, who won. Democrat Chris Bell got 30 percent, while Strayhorn tallied 18 percent. Friedman, an irreverent independent with libertarian impulses, received 12 percent of the vote. Before he resumed his old life, Friedman gave voice to the frustrations of independents everywhere. "This is a chance for people to triumph over politics," he said. "This is not about Rick Perry or Carole Strayhorn. It's about changing politics itself—and politics itself sucks."[4]

On that Amtrak call, I learned just how much truth was in Kinky Friedman's pithy summation. Jonathan informed me that he had failed to meet the minimum signature threshold. His petition-gathering firm had fraudulently overrepresented the number of signatures that they had collected.[5] By the time he and his team figured out what was going on, it was too late. He had built an impressive campaign team and invested considerable money into the race, and tens of thousands of Texans wanted him on the ballot. Yet Jonathan's race was over before it really began. His name would not appear on the ballot in November.

Ballot Access Fallacies

In a constitutional democracy, it should be a basic right of all citizens to run for elective office—and for voters to be able to pull the lever for the candidate of their choice, even if those candidates lack a *D* or an *R* after their names. While it is reasonable to have some test of the legitimacy of a candidate so the ballot isn't completely unwieldy, any restrictions should be the minimum needed to ensure the efficient function of our electoral process. This is not the case in our country. Getting on the ballot in Maryland is not nearly as difficult as it is in Texas, but in my state, unless you are a Republican or a Democrat, it still takes ten thousand signatures.

The reigning political elites offer two justifications for engineering such obstacles to being listed on the ballot. Both are spurious.

Their primary motivation, which they don't hide, is to protect the two-party system. Their presumption is that the existing arrangement adds stability to our democracy, whereas multiparty legislative bodies create chaos. Considering the grotesque gridlock our current two-party structure has brought to Capitol Hill, this is laughable. It's also bad history. The nation's founders mistrusted political parties and never envisioned a permanent duopoly.[6] Even if you accept the logic of a two-party system, which I don't, the obstacles in the way of minority parties and unaffiliated candidates stymie the normal evolutionary process by which a sclerotic party dies out and is replaced by a dynamic new party with fresh ideas.

In nineteenth century America, four U.S. presidents were Whig Party members. A pro-business, small-government party, its time had passed. Whigs opposed western expansion and didn't see slavery as a crisis. Missing the boat on the two great issues of the day rendered Whigs obsolete. So they were replaced by a dynamic new political party led by Abraham Lincoln. That could not have happened without open access to the ballot box. The presidential election of 1860 featured four viable candidates and produced, arguably, the greatest president in U.S. history.*

A result like that would be unlikely today. Not only are independents and third-party candidates denied admittance to the all-important television debates, as we discussed in chapter 2, unless they are billionaires (like Ross Perot, who died while I was writing this chapter), it's nearly impossible to gather signatures and meet other requirements

---

* The lessons of 1860 must be learned anew by succeeding generations of Americans. Nearly a century after Lincoln's selection, the U.S. Supreme Court acknowledged as much in a 1957 case called *Sweezy v. New Hampshire*. Seeking to root Communists out of New Hampshire's university system, state attorney general Louis C. Wyman questioned Marxist college professor Paul Sweezy about his economic theories and influences. Sweezy declined to answer and was found in contempt. On appeal, Sweezy's refusal was backed by the U.S. Supreme Court. "All political ideas cannot and should not be channeled into the programs of our two major parties," wrote Chief Justice Earl Warren. "History has amply proved the virtue of political activity by minority, dissident groups, who innumerable times have been in the vanguard of democratic thought and whose programs were ultimately accepted...The absence of such voices would be a symptom of grave illness in our society."

to get on the presidential ballot in all fifty states.

The second tenet espoused by the duopoly to rationalize restrictive ballot rules is that too many candidates would confuse voters. "Imagine, if there were fifty candidates on a ballot," they exclaim, "the election would be a farce!" This is a canard and has been disproven repeatedly.

In states with more lenient ballot requirements, you do get more candidates, but not a stampede.[7] Richard Winger, the nation's leading expert in the field, has researched races for partisan statewide office in every one of the fifty states. In all of U.S. history, he found, when a state required more than five thousand signatures, there has never been a government-printed ballot with more than eight names on the ballot.[8]

Yet in eighteen states, more signatures are required, sometimes many more. Florida's formula requires independent or minor party presidential candidates to collect more than one hundred thousand signatures, for example. In North Carolina, the number in 2020 will be 70,666, although a minority party candidate could get on the ballot with 11,778. If you wonder why North Carolina officials favor minor party candidates over independents, there is not a satisfying answer. Some of these laws are just an irrational hodgepodge. Even when states seek to address it in good faith, they don't always get it right. In Oklahoma, a 2020 independent candidate would have to collect 43,590 signatures. But the state recently added an option of paying a $35,000 filing fee instead, which at least gives candidates another avenue to compete.

If I had run four years earlier, it would have been forty thousand in Maryland. The law was changed when Greg Dorsey, an independent Senate candidate, went to court with help from Richard Winger.[9] When a trial court judge issued a preliminary ruling in Dorsey's favor, the state board of elections announced it would not enforce the higher standard. The legislature made the change to ten thousand names, and Republican governor Larry Hogan let it become law in 2017 without his signature.* Yet I still had to get ten thousand voters to sign my petition. And as I learned, that's a lot, especially when state officials are digging deep in their bag of tricks to keep you off the ballot.

A "Rose" by Any Other Name

If you lived in Maryland and were approached by an enthusiastic individual carrying a clipboard in the spring and summer of 2018, it was almost certainly someone from my campaign. These people, mainly college students working while home for summer break, approached strangers saying, "Hi. Are you a Maryland voter?" In order to get me on November's ballot, we needed the signatures by August 6.

Unlike party-affiliated candidates, who merely write a small check to the board of elections to participate in the electoral process, independent candidates secure their place on the ballot the old-fashioned way. I am not exaggerating. In the age of automatic or online voter registration, petitioning for ballot access in Maryland can only be done with pen and paper. As in Texas, political insiders designed the process to make it difficult to run. A valid petition requires much more information than simply signing a piece of paper. The form requires the exact name in which the signer is registered to vote, the address where they are registered, the date the voter signed the petition, as well as their date of birth. In a climate of fear about identity theft, thousands of people who indicated they wanted me to run refused, out of caution, to provide

---

* The governor did sign my petition, however. I had met Hogan several times during the campaign and consider him a model politician who puts our state's needs above the interests of his party. He signed our petition at the Tawes Clam Bake in Crisfield, a town on Maryland's Eastern Shore. A week before the election, he told me that he was going to vote for me. I was prouder of that than getting his signature.

anything beyond their name and signature.

Additionally, our volunteers were often stopped by security personnel at universities and public parks, sometimes by law enforcement officers. After consulting with the Center for Competitive Democracy, which confirmed that ballot petitioning in the public square is a basic First Amendment right, we provided our team documents to show in the event they were confronted. Even then, there were places where my team was forcibly told to leave public places. It took our petition team over three months to secure enough signatures to make an initial submission to the state board in Annapolis. In the heat of summer, we spent hundreds of hours outdoors, engaging thousands of Marylanders every day. We visited college campuses, local community events, grocery store parking lots, and our favorite spot, Camden Yards Stadium. On July 19, six of us climbed into my campaign RV and hand-carried a dozen heavy boxes containing 12,073 signatures into the Maryland State Board of Elections office on West Street in Annapolis.

Most campaigns employ professional petition-gathering firms to collect signatures, but we accomplished the feat entirely on our own. Most of the work was done by nineteen passionate campaign fellows, college students who believe that our political system is broken and were willing to work to do something about it.* Unfortunately, the board of

---

* I'd be remiss in not thanking these dedicated volunteers by name: Nick Abushacra, Northwestern University; Idris Ali, Catholic University of America; Ben Birnbach, University of Maryland; Will Burns, University of St. Andrews; Gabrielle Cecchi, Fordham University; Francisco Flores-Pourrat, Catholic University of America; Samantha Frenkel-Poppell, Harvard University; Oliver Goodman, Johns Hopkins University; Grace Hotung, Towson University; Eduardo Leal, Catholic University of America; Omar Qureshi, Catholic University of America; Matthew McDonald, St. Mary's University; Alec Samuels, Vanderbilt University; Jake Simon, Brown University; Emily Snyder, Catholic University of America; Dean Suozzi-Auberry, Catholic University of America; Chaz Vest, Brown University; Jessica Vincent, Indiana University; Peter Zaudtke, University of St. Andrews.

elections had other ideas. In Maryland, the board verifies each individual signature and provides daily updates on their verification process. Knowing that some signatures would be invalidated due to unidentifiable handwriting or other reasons, we projected a loss rate of 25 percent and planned to submit an additional two thousand signatures to give ourselves a cushion. After a few days of verification reports, we realized the board of elections was eliminating more than 40 percent of our signatures, frustrating our team and creating uncertainty as the August deadline loomed.

The most common reason for the invalidation of signatures was "name standard." If a voter completed the form but hadn't written their name *exactly* as it appeared on the state's voter registration roll, the signature was rejected. For example, a voter's registration might include a middle name that was omitted on the petition form. Or someone may have signed "Matt" instead of "Matthew" or perhaps "Jane B. Rose" instead of "Jane Rose." Although it would have been easy to confirm the validity of these signatures, the state refused to count them. This is more than government officials behaving pedantically. It's institutionalized bad faith.

With relentless effort, we collected an additional five thousand signatures that we dropped off a few hours before the 5:00 p.m. August 6 deadline. A few days later, we were officially notified that we had cleared the threshold and that my name would appear on the November ballot. Although my campaign prevailed, it came at a cost. We had unexpectedly been forced to invest hundreds of extra people-hours on petitioning, while other campaign activities were put on hold.

Bruce A. Johnson, a fellow independent candidate in Maryland, was not as lucky. Bruce is an African American trial lawyer who was running for state's attorney in Prince George's County. I first met him while gathering signatures in Bowie at a Memorial Day parade. Clad in a suit and tie on an eighty-five-degree day, Bruce worked the crowd collecting signatures. In the deeply blue county, he was challenging a popular Democrat. He knew he was an underdog but wanted to provide voters with an independent option in the general election.

As our paths crossed often on the campaign trail, I came to admire Bruce's integrity, belief in public service, and willingness to defy the two-party orthodoxy. In early August, knowing how hard he'd worked to collect signatures, I was thrilled to learn that he had successfully submitted the required number before the deadline. My elation was short-lived. The board of elections, applying the same cynical standards that they did on my petition, invalidated large numbers of his signatures and rejected Bruce's petition, despite the wishes of thousands of residents of PG County. With no time left, Bruce filed suit, to no avail. His name was left off the ballot.[10]

Another Type of Identity Politics

It's not only independent candidates and voters who are gamed by election officials. So are Republicans in predominantly Democratic states and Democrats in predominantly Republican states. Stacey Abrams, a Democrat who ran for governor in Republican-controlled Georgia in 2018, learned this bitter lesson. In a first-person New York Times opinion piece, she described running into the state's "exact match" policy—the same scam that knocked Bruce Johnson off the ballot and nearly did the same to me.[11] In Georgia, fifty-three thousand voter registrations were "held hostage" because the names did not match exactly between voter registration and driver's licenses. The example Abrams cited was a last name listed as "del Rio" on the voter files but as "delRio" with the DMV.

Abrams wrote that local and state officials across the country are "shamelessly weakening voter registration, ballot access and ballot-counting procedures." I agree entirely. But while Abrams's comments were targeted toward Georgia Republicans, her own party uses the same tactics to prevent competition from independents in Maryland and other states around the country.

The most outrageous example was the fury unleashed on Ralph Nader when the then-seventy-year-old liberal reformer decided to run for president in 2004. A hero to progressives since his legendary battles with General Motors in the 1960s, Nader had become a pariah among liberal activists, who blamed his 2000 presidential candidacy for Al Gore's loss to George W. Bush. Determined to give John Kerry a clear shot at Bush, party bosses conspired to keep Nader off the 2004 ballot. As soon as his supporters began their petition drives, Democratic lawyers challenged the signatures, ultimately keeping his name off the ballot in Pennsylvania, Oregon, Virginia, Ohio, and other swing states.[12] The methods used against Nader were also vindictive on a personal level and in some cases illegal.[13]

In Oregon, Kerry surrogate Howard Dean publicly accused Nader's supporters of teaming up with "right-wing, anti-gay Republicans."[14] Dean followed up on this slur by encouraging Oregon Democrats to shun gatherings where Nader sought to gather signatures. Under Oregon law, a third-party candidate can get on the ballot by holding a convention at which one thousand registered voters sign a petition. Oregon Democrats didn't merely boycott those meetings; they sabotaged them. Organized by state party officials in Portland, they packed Nader's event until the convention hall was full—keeping out actual Nader supporters—and then didn't sign the petition. This happened twice. Undaunted, Nader's forces went the other route, collecting signatures one at a time. They submitted more than twenty-eight thousand names to state officials, nearly twice the required number. Of these, 18,186 were validated by Oregon's Board of Elections. You can guess what happened next. Secretary of State Bill Bradbury, a career Democratic politician, used criteria written nowhere in state law to invalidate three thousand more signatures. If petition pages were misnumbered, he threw out whole pages of signatures. When he was done, the Nader forces came up 218 signatures short.[15]

What happened in Pennsylvania was even nastier. There, Nader submitted forty-seven thousand signatures, far more than the required 25,697. The partisan machine went into overdrive. Democratic lawyers sued to keep Nader off the ballot because he was a Reform Party candidate in a few other states.[16] This facile legal theory was affirmed by Democratic jurists—in Pennsylvania judges are elected officials—who wrote: "In Pennsylvania, candidates seeking to appear on the ballot as independents may not have sought nomination by a political body in the same election cycle."*

Actually, this law applies to election cycles *within* Pennsylvania, and the state Supreme Court overturned it. Meanwhile, Democratic state employees had been working overtime, literally at taxpayer expense, searching for irregularities in the signatures. (Yes, paying public employees to do this was illegal, and people went to prison for it. But it didn't help Nader.) Using the typical gimmicks—tossing signatures signed "Bill" for someone registered to vote as "William"—Nader was kept off the ballot. Not content with their victory, Democratic lawyers demanded that Nader pay the fees they incurred while keeping him off the ballot, some $81,000.[17]

---

* Judges in Pennsylvania are no more nonpartisan than the secretary of state's office in Oregon. In 2010, the judge who wrote the overturned anti-Nader decision ran for statewide office as a Democrat in Pennsylvania. In Oregon, Bill Bradbury did the same thing in the same year. Neither won.

"Ralph Nader became the first candidate in American history to be penalized financially by a state for attempting to run for public office," Oliver Hall, the lawyer who has represented Nader since 2005, told me.[18] Fresh out of law school when he took this case, Oliver was so appalled by what he found that he started a nonprofit, the Center for Competitive Democracy. Most disturbing to reformers was the brazenness of the partisan politicians fighting to restrict Americans' choices at the ballot box.

"I wanted to prevent Ralph Nader from doing what he did in Florida in 2000," Gregory Harvey, the Philadelphia lawyer who led the anti-Nader crusade, told reporters. Former state party chairman T. J. Rooney couldn't hide his glee at the harassment of Nader. "You're goddamned right he should pay," Rooney said. "And he should go away, because he didn't learn his lesson in 2000."[19]

The "lesson," according to the keepers of the duopoly, is that Americans' right to run for elective office doesn't really exist unless they have *R* or *D* after their names—and that voters who want more than two choices on Election Day should live somewhere other than the United States.

Nader and Oliver Hall have spent more fighting the judgment than the $81,000 would have cost. But they believe, as I do, that the principle of ballot access is worth fighting for. "Yes, I can afford it," Nader told McClatchy Newspapers. "But the necessity of a diversified electoral process can't afford it."[20]

International Outlier

Until 1948, more than half the states in the country permitted candidates on the ballot with one thousand signatures or fewer. To keep third parties off the ballots, some states began erecting hurdles. These measures had nothing to do with avoiding voter confusion or protecting democracy; they were mechanisms to prevent challenges from political movements ranging from the "Dixiecrats" on the right to socialist parties on the left. When George Wallace's presidential candidacy threatened their dominance in 1968, the duopoly doubled down on their efforts to restrict ballot access.

A challenge to these machinations arose in Ohio, which had enacted measures designed to keep Wallace's American Independent Party and the Socialist Labor Party off the ballot. Ohio's new law required new party candidates to submit 433,100 signatures by February in an election year. Wallace's party gathered that many signatures but missed the deadline. The Socialists, who had been on the Ohio ballot until 1948, failed to gather the requisite signatures. The U.S. Supreme Court ruled that Ohio had unconstitutionally burdened the rights of voters and candidates. Ohio's scheme, the court ruled, gave Republican and Democratic candidates "a permanent monopoly on the right to have people vote for or against them."[21]

The Warren Court made several other rulings to protect minority voting rights: declaring poll taxes unconstitutional, striking down property ownership requirements for voters, and upholding the Voting Rights Act of 1965. A few years later, however, things took a turn for the worse. In 1971, under Chief Justice Warren Burger, the court ruled against the Socialist Workers Party in a case called *Jenness v. Fortson*. Linda Jenness, like Stacey Abrams, was a Georgia gubernatorial candidate. Unlike Abrams, she was required to obtain 88,175 signatures to be on the ballot. Under Georgia law, each petition had to be notarized and submitted by mid-June, and the signature collectors needed to be registered voters in the area where the petitions were circulated. The high court, clueless as to the difficulty to meeting these requirements, adjudged Georgia's standard reasonable. In a scathing rebuttal in the *Election Law Journal*, Richard Winger argued convincingly that "all six of the conclusions that the Court drew about Georgia's ballot access laws, and about ballot access laws in general, were either based on factual error, or ignored important factual information."[22]

After *Jenness*, the two-party regime became bolder. Two years later, Oklahoma increased its signature requirement eightfold, despite having no history of crowded ballots. In Texas, the hurdles keep getting higher for independent candidates. The state's requirement will rise to eighty thousand signatures in 2020.

The branch of government that should smack down the duopoly is the judiciary. The problem is that courts continue to ignore the difference between *bipartisan* and *nonpartisan* behavior. This is a common misconception. I first learned about duopolies and how they behave as an economics student at Brown University and later at the University of Chicago's business school. Absent regulation of their behavior, duopolists build barriers to new competition. Their impact can be more pernicious and harder to uproot than monopolies because competition between two enterprises creates the illusion of an open marketplace. We are accustomed to the term *bipartisan* being a sign of constructive compromise. And it can mean that. But, when it comes to ballot access, bipartisan is synonymous with duopolistic collusion in restraint of democracy. *Nonpartisan* would mean establishing rules that create no partisan advantage, even for the two major parties.

In 2016, when presidential candidates Hillary Clinton and Donald Trump combined for record negative poll ratings, Evan McMullin emerged as an independent contender.[23] McMullin was a former CIA operations officer, investment banker, and advisor to the House Committee on Foreign Affairs. He was a credible candidate whose best showing was in Utah, where he ended up with 22 percent of the vote, only six points behind Clinton. McMullin's campaign manager was Joel Searby, who would help me launch my campaign two years later. According to Joel, McMullin didn't start his campaign until August 8, 2016, and for the first six weeks, 80 percent of the team's time was consumed by collecting signatures to get on the ballots. McMullin ended up qualifying in only eleven states.

Other countries have taken notice. The Organization for Security and Cooperation in Europe has issued reports critical of our ballot access laws, suggesting the United States is in violation of the Copenhagen Document, signed by President George H. W. Bush as part of the Helsinki Accords. The OSCE report specifically mentioned the right of citizens to seek public office, individually or as representatives of political parties, without discrimination.[24] Most other countries ensure these rights by having permanent, autonomous, nonpartisan election commissions that insulate election administration from partisan politics. The United States, on the other hand, allows party-affiliated officials to administer elections. The nation that gave representative democracy to the world now bewilders other countries by using undemocratic election practices that our own Founding Fathers would have rejected.

Bad Candidates Make Bad Law

Ballot access is not a sexy topic, which is why partisan elites can get away with so much. One member of Congress who does care is Republican-turned-independent Justin Amash of Michigan. Even before he broke with Donald Trump and his party, Amash proposed the Ballot Fairness Act, which would eliminate straight ticket voting and require major party candidates to meet the same ballot access standards as independents. "Laws should not advantage particular political parties or discriminate against candidates who choose not to affiliate with a party," he said.[25]

The first Republican member to call for President Trump's impeachment, Amash isn't afraid to speak the truth. But less scrupulous politicians, aided and abetted by their allies in the press, have used antipathy for Trump as an excuse to attack anyone who threatens the duopoly. When Howard Schultz began talking about running for president in 2020, he was met with a torrent of abuse from Democrats[26] and media elites, all of which could be distilled into a single primal scream: "How dare you?"[27]

It's the same question asked of Ralph Nader in 2000 and 2004. The answer is fundamental. I know because I had to answer it for myself when I ran for the Senate: I "dared" to run because the two major parties have come to represent mainly their donors and the hyperpartisan activists on the extreme wings of the nation's ideological spectrum. And because it's my birthright as an American.

Item 6 of the Contract to Unite America contains two provisions to prevent partisan insiders from abusing the ballot qualifying process. The first is to mandate that the same standards apply to all candidates: independents, those from minor parties, and those from the two major parties. All candidates would be created equal. The second calls for a ceiling of five thousand signatures that can be required on a petition for ballot access. That is still a challenge and would weed out those who want to file for office as a lark. Two-thirds of Americans want a third party or independent option in elections, and partisan ideologues should no longer control who gets to run for office.[28]

Meanwhile, the duopoly is trying to take the country in the opposite direction. In late July, California governor Gavin Newsom signed a law passed by Democrats in the state legislature barring Trump from the ballot in the 2020 Republican primary unless he releases his tax returns.[29] While I believe presidential candidates should release their tax returns—and Trump has lied repeatedly about his intentions—this law is undemocratic in the worst ways. It violates the California State Constitution and probably the U.S. Constitution as well, and is contemptuous of the 63 million Americans (4.5 million of them Californians) who voted for Trump in 2016. What troubles me most is the mind-set it reveals: that voting is not a right but instead a privilege that can be conferred, and revoked, by hyperpartisan politicians on a whim. If replicated, this would undermine democracy itself. If California does that, why shouldn't Texas Republicans keep Joe Biden off the ballot for some GOP grievance, such as the former vice president's promise that under Obamacare, Americans could keep their health plans?

Of course, I don't want to give Texas Republicans any more ideas about limiting ballot access. As GOP legislators in Austin contemplated new ballot barriers, Oliver Hall filed suit against Texas. "You have a dead-end on the political process," Oliver explained. "There's no capacity for innovation, there's no ability for new voices to come onto the scene and present alternatives in terms of new ideas."[30]

Contract Item 7

FAIR DISTRICTS ACT:

Each state will form an independent commission
responsible for redistricting. Political affiliation can
no longer be considered when drawing districts.

Mickey Mouse Maps and
Goofy Districts

A few weeks prior to the election, on a Saturday morning in mid-October 2018, I found myself in Oakland, Maryland. My team and I were there to meet local leaders and walk in the town's annual Autumn Glory parade. Nestled in the far western corner of the state, Oakland is set at an altitude of 2,400 feet, near the Wisp ski resort. On this early autumn day, the temperature was in the thirties, and it was sleeting. Oakland is the seat of Garrett County, where 70 percent of voters are registered Republicans, which makes it a world away politically from where I live in liberal Montgomery County.

To get there we had traveled two hundred miles from home, about as far as you can go while remaining in the state of Maryland, which is why I was surprised to run into my neighbor David Trone. David lives a mile from me and was running for one of Maryland's eight seats in the U.S. House of Representatives. I had momentarily forgotten that, since the 2011 redistricting, a thin strip of populous Montgomery County was included in Maryland's Sixth Congressional District, which spanned all the way to the state's western border. So, like me, Trone was running to represent the people of Oakland.

Until 2012, the district had been represented for twenty years by

Republican Roscoe Bartlett. Western Maryland is conservative, and Bartlett had won ten consecutive terms, typically by margins of 20 percent or more. Then the Democrats in Annapolis started playing with maps.[1]

Under Governor Martin O'Malley, Maryland's districts were reconfigured after the 2010 census. The Sixth District was contorted to include a highly liberal slice of Montgomery County, giving it a Democratic majority. Before election day 2010, the district included 208,000 Republicans and 160,000 Democrats. Two years later, it was 146,000 Republicans and 193,000 Democrats. O'Malley's mapmaking had an explicit goal: to get seven of the state's eight House seats in Democratic hands. Years later, the former governor admitted first under oath during litigation and then publicly that he and Maryland's six House Democrats, including congressional leader Steny Hoyer, called their plan the "7–1 Map."[2] Writing in USA Today, O'Malley justified the shameless power play as retaliation for years of similar shenanigans by Republicans in other states. "I responded to GOP gerrymandering with my own," he said, no longer bothering with the charade that the redistricting was fair to Maryland voters.[3]

The scheme worked. In 2012, after twenty years in office, Bartlett was defeated by Democrat John Delaney, and Democrats took their seventh seat in Maryland's congressional delegation.

Cracking and Packing

As most politically astute Americans know, this process of redrawing district lines for political advantage—"gerrymandering" as it's called—is not new. The term dates back to 1812 after Massachusetts governor Elbridge Gerry shamelessly redrew the state's legislative election districts

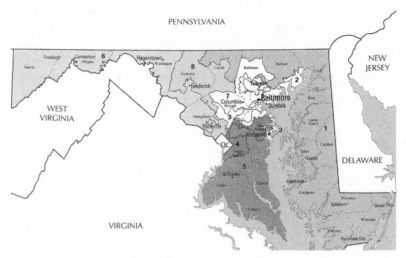

Map of Maryland's Congressional Districts

to disadvantage the Federalist Party and help his own party.* One state senate district in particular resembled a reptile, proving irresistible to satirists at the time. ("Gerrymander" is a combination of the governor's name and the word "salamander.")[4] Much has been written about this problem over the years, but the basics never change. Once every ten years, after the U.S. Census, states are required by the Constitution to draw new voting districts to reflect population shifts. The process, controlled by the legislature in most states, creates an opportunity for the majority party to game the system for its own advantage.

Gerrymandering entails two main tactics. The first, called "cracking," involves spreading the voters from the minority party across many districts in order to dilute the power of that party and give an electoral

---

* Gerry's party was officially called the Democratic-Republican Party. Founded by Thomas Jefferson and James Madison, it was usually called the Republican Party at the time—although it's the forerunner of today's Democratic Party. If that sounds confusing, it's fitting: both of today's major political parties have consistently used gerrymandering to skew American politics.

advantage to the majority party in as many jurisdictions as possible. This is what happened to the conservative electorate of Maryland's Sixth District. The voters who had supported Roscoe Bartlett for two decades were dispersed among three congressional districts.[5]

The second main strategy, used when the minority party's membership is too large to dissipate entirely, is to pack as many of those voters as possible into one district to contain their impact. The idea is to cause the minority party to "waste" votes on elections they win by landslides. This method, called "packing," is what happened in Maryland's First Congressional District. The 2012 O'Malley-led gerrymander concentrated as many Republicans as possible into that jurisdiction, forming another bizarrely shaped district. Republican Andy Harris has been in office since then, typically winning the general election by over 30 percent.[6]

In 2018, Harris was confronted by a capable and moderate Democratic challenger named Jesse Colvin. Normally, in such a "wave" midterm election year, Colvin would have been a good bet to attract enough centrists' support to be competitive.[7] He opposed Medicare for All, ran against Washington hyperpartisanship, and even reached out to me for help with independents. None of it mattered. In a district literally "packed" with every Maryland Republican the Democrats could squeeze in, Harris won by 22 percent.

Extreme Maps Mean Extreme Politicians

When districts like Maryland's First are reconfigured to be a "lock" for one party, the general election becomes unimportant, and the only race that matters is the majority party's primary. After winning Maryland's First Congressional District seat, Andy Harris joined the Freedom Caucus, a group of Republican members so conservative that they drove Republican House Speaker John Boehner out of public life. Harris has since been reelected three times in a district where the only challenge he ever has to worry about is from the right. This is how a liberal state like Maryland ends up with an ultraconservative as its only Republican representative in Congress—and how gerrymandering feeds Washington's toxic culture.

What would be the makeup of the Maryland delegation, if the lines were drawn fairly? Well, my state has some four million registered voters. Eighteen percent are, like me, independents. Of the remainder, Democrats outnumber Republicans 2–1. In a 2018 poll conducted by McLaughlin & Associates for my campaign, we found that 31 percent of Marylanders labeled themselves as liberal, 37 percent as moderate, and 32 percent as conservative. So the answer is that, if my state's eight House seats were divided proportionally to the electorate, our congressional delegation would most likely consist of two liberal Democrats and two conservative Republicans, along with three center-left Democrats and one moderate independent. Instead, with gerrymandered districts, the state is represented by seven Democrats, who vote reliably with the party leadership, and one far-right Republican.

Gerrymandering has other insidious effects as well. In certain districts, it makes it more difficult for those elected to represent the diverse interests of their constituents. I thought about this in Oakland when I ran into David Trone, my neighbor who ended up winning his race. Trone is somehow supposed to simultaneously represent the interests of (a) conservative, rural Garrett County, (b) Hagerstown with its shrinking population and opioid crisis, and (c) very liberal and wealthy suburbs of Washington, D.C., in Montgomery County. This would be difficult for anyone, regardless of political party. No wonder Congress's approval rating is so low.

Maryland is in no way unique. Nationally, districts have been reconfigured to the point where almost all House races are easy wins for one party or the other. Even in the 2018 midterms, when Democrats recaptured a majority in the House, only 75 out of the 435 races were deemed competitive by the *Cook Political Report*.[8]

In recent years, Republicans have been devastatingly effective at gerrymandering in swing states. In Ohio, where party registration is closely split and political control has traditionally oscillated between the two parties, Republicans now hold twelve of sixteen House seats (75 percent). In the "purple" state of North Carolina, as this book was being written, Democrats claimed only three of the state's thirteen congressional seats.

What are the results of this con game? When they are being honest, even longtime incumbents who personally benefit from gerrymandering will admit how it warps our governance. "The damage done by gerrymandering isn't difficult to measure," wrote Marcy Kaptur, Ohio's longest-serving member of Congress, in a revealing 2019 op-ed. "It breeds partisan legislators, who in turn breed a partisan Congress. Gerrymandering has made virtually all House seats safer—including mine—and the members who hold those safe seats are often less responsive to communities and unwilling to compromise in Washington."[9]

In 1982, when Kaptur was first elected, the now-lopsided Ohio congressional delegation was virtually even: ten Democrats and eleven Republicans. And although the size of the delegation is smaller now, Buckeye State voting patterns haven't changed much over the years. Barack Obama carried Ohio twice, but Donald Trump won the state in 2016. In the 2018 congressional midterms, 2.3 million Ohioans voted for a Republican, compared to slightly more than 2 million who voted for a Democrat. Yet those 2 million votes produced only four Democratic members compared to eight Republican seats.

"We all know the culprit," Kaptur added. "Radical, partisan

gerrymandering. The result is both the decay of our national discourse and the failure of our institutions to fulfill their most basic functions."[10]

Many influential Republicans agree. GOP advocates for reform include Maryland's governor, Larry Hogan, and Arnold Schwarzenegger, the former governor of California. As far back as the 1980s, Ronald Reagan called for "an end to the anti-democratic and un-American practice of gerrymandering congressional districts."

"The fact is gerrymandering has become a national scandal," Reagan added in a 1987 speech on political reform. "A look at the district lines shows how corrupt the whole process has become. The congressional map is a horror show of grotesque, contorted shapes. Districts jump back and forth over mountain ranges, cross large bodies of water, send out little tentacles to absorb special communities and ensure safe seats. One Democratic congressman who helped engineer the gerrymandering of California once described the district lines there as his contribution to modern art."[11]

Reagan was referring to Phillip Burton, the legendary San Francisco political boss who drew the state's voting map in 1981, giving Democrats a 28–17 margin in House seats—in an evenly divided state Reagan had carried twice. Phil Burton was brazen about it, too, to the point of carving out a district for his own brother.[12] "It's my contribution to modern art," Burton crowed.[13] "It's gorgeous. It curls in and out like a snake."* Reagan's outrage is worth remembering because although redistricting reform is more popular among Democrats than Republicans today, it was once reversed. The point is that each party uses this cartographic weapon when they have the power.

---

* Serpentine metaphors have been a recurring theme since the original "Gerry Mander." In 2012, when Ohio Republicans tossed Democrats Marcy Kaptur and Dennis Kucinich in the same district, the new congressional district was derisively nicknamed "the Snake by the Lake."

Self-Segregation

While gerrymandering contributes to the polarization of the electorate, it is not the only cause. There are other factors, including the recent trend of Americans organizing ourselves into politically homogenous communities, a process described in an influential 2008 book by Bill Bishop, *The Big Sort: Why the Clustering of Like-Minded America Is Tearing Us Apart*.[14]

Americans are sorted geographically along partisan lines more than ever. According to respected political analyst David Wasserman, from 1992 to 2016, in the nation's 3,113 counties (or county equivalents), the number of county elections decided by less than 10 percent declined from 1,096 to 303. During the same period, the number of "landslide" counties, those decided by at least 50 percent, exploded from 93 to 1,196. Wasserman, the U.S. House Editor for the *Cook Political Report*, goes on to show that from 1992 to 2016, the share of voters living in landslide counties quintupled from 4 percent to 21 percent.[15] County borders have not changed, so gerrymandering does not explain these growing disparities. This happened as the two major parties began to arrange themselves in a more linear fashion along public policy lines: conservatives gravitated toward the Republican Party and liberals to the Democratic Party, a development described by political scientists William Galston and Elaine C. Kamarck as "the great sorting-out of the electorate."[16]

The Voting Rights Act and its amendments had unintended consequences. The landmark civil rights legislation outlawed despicable Jim Crow electoral practices in the South but ultimately also skewed the distribution of voters. When Congress amended the law in 1982, it effectively mandated the packing of minorities, whenever possible, into "majority-minority" districts. New lines were drawn that linked widely separated black communities, and it had the intended result. For the first time in a hundred years, African Americans were elected to the House of Representatives from Alabama, Florida, North Carolina, South Carolina, and Virginia. However, the packing of black voters, who are overwhelmingly Democrats, into specific districts also led to the election of more Republicans in the remaining parts of these states. This provision of the Voting Rights Act, championed by Democrats, may as well have been called "The Help Restore the Republicans in the South Act."[17]

When you add it all up—gerrymandering, self-sorting, and the impact of "majority-minority" racial districts—you end up with general elections with predetermined results. If you define a competitive election as one decided by 5 percent or less, then few of our House races fit the bill. In 2014 only 31 of the 435 races were competitive (7 percent of total). In 2016 it was 22 races (5 percent), and in 2018, 45 races (10 percent). And it's poised to get worse.

Partisan gerrymandering has been weaponized by computers and data analytics. It was only a few censuses ago that politicians were using paper maps and markers to draw district lines. After the 2010 election, party bosses used computers to assist their cartography. Ten years later, the publicly available information is many times more granular and can be used to create highly accurate "partisan strength indexes." In a nutshell, political experts probably have a better idea of how you will vote in 2020 than you do. When it comes to gerrymandering, the last consequential election was in 2010, when Republicans secured legislative majorities in North Carolina, Pennsylvania, and Wisconsin, among others, and pressed their advantage in electoral maps. The next redistricting will be done after the 2020 census. Today's virulent political environment virtually guarantees it will be a horror show.

How Should We Draw the Lines?

If we want to improve our redistricting process, the first step is determining on what basis districts should be drawn. While meeting the legal requirements for contiguity and population, the criteria should include:

+ *Geographic compactness:* No more cynically drawn districts evocative of reptilian metaphors.

+ *Natural boundaries:* Don't capriciously divide up cities, counties, and towns.

+ *Population density:* Use consistent formulas—not partisan objectives—to determine congressional boundaries.

+ *Demographic diversity:* Don't disperse racial or ethnic groups in ways that dilute their representation in Congress.

+ *Voting Rights Act:* Prohibit the manipulation of this iconic law for partisan advantage.

There is one criterion used in some jurisdictions that I believe should *never* be considered: political competitiveness. Arizona's independent redistricting commission, for example, is tasked to ensure the competitiveness of elections. To me, this is a classic example of the Law of Unintended Consequences. Its well-intentioned objective is to dilute the power of the left and right wings in the two major parties and increase the importance of the general election. To do this, Arizona mapmakers sought to maximize the number of districts evenly split between Republicans and Democrats. It's an appealing aim but a temptation to be resisted. All this really does is set in concrete the wrong-headed idea that congressional maps are puzzles to be rigged and manipulated. Most of the reform commissions that have studied gerrymandering agree with me. District boundaries should be drawn to make sure citizens are fairly represented and should never be drawn with specific election outcomes in mind.

The United States is one of the few countries in the world that leaves redistricting to partisan legislatures, with results that leave some voters bewildered, and others—those who know how it's done—embittered. Take the election cycle of 2012, for instance. President Obama carried all the "swing" states while prevailing in the Electoral College 332–206 and winning the popular vote by nearly five million votes. Meanwhile Democrats picked up two more Senate seats, solidifying their hold on the upper chamber, and Democratic candidates for the House tallied 1.4 million more votes than GOP congressional candidates. Yet when the dust cleared, Republicans easily retained control of the House. How did they do it? To enterprising journalist-turned-reformer David Daley, the answer, which he detailed in a well-received 2016 book, *Ratf**ked: How the Democrats Won the Presidency but Lost America*, was alarming. In 2010, operating below the radar and using dark money, top GOP operatives implemented an ambitious plan called REDMAP with a mind toward further carving up the congressional map in ways that benefited Republicans. Employing ruthless campaign consultants unburdened by any obligation to campaign fairly, they targeted vulnerable Democratic state legislators in key states, all with a mind toward controlling who would draw the maps after the 2010 census.[18] After 2012, it was clear just how successful they'd been—if one can count success as making the "people's House" even more hyperpartisan and unrepresentative than it was before.

Americans are wise to this scam, even if they don't know how to stop it. According to a poll done by ALG Research, over two-thirds of Americans are now familiar with the term gerrymandering and view it overwhelmingly negatively.[19] Voters from both parties want to end gerrymandering, including 65 percent of Republicans and 80 percent of Democrats. During my campaign, I never met a voter who disagreed.

No Relief in the Courts

Until 2019, the courts were an active battlefield in the fight against gerrymandering. The Supreme Court had determined that extreme partisan map drawing could be unconstitutional but had not established a standard to measure it. That left the question open to lower federal courts and state courts to decide as the lawsuits piled up. The legal challenges showed that not much had changed since the 1812 "Gerry Mander" or the 2012 "Snake by the Lake."

Pennsylvania's Seventh Congressional District, for instance, was comically distorted. To create a safe Republican seat, the legislature drew lines that became the poster child for excess partisanship. State senator Andy Dinniman announced a tongue-in-cheek contest to name the new district, a competition won unofficially by David Daley, who hilariously dubbed it "Goofy Kicking Donald Duck."[20] The state Supreme Court apparently agreed, ruling that the boundaries violated the state's constitution.[21] A new voting map was put in place for the 2018 election.

And so it went around the country, a patchwork of decisions that begged a resolution by the U.S. Supreme Court. A federal court in Wisconsin ruled that districts had been drawn in a way to intentionally disadvantage one party and required the lines to be redrawn. There

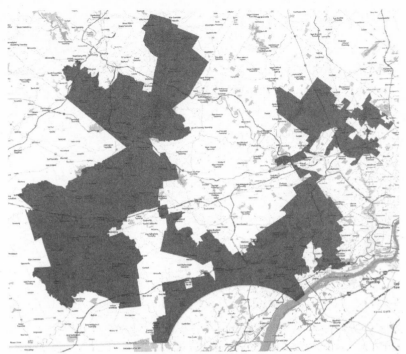

Pennsylvania's Seventh District until 2018. Courtesy of Daniel McGlone, Azavea.

were also challenges to partisan maps in Florida, Illinois, Maryland, Michigan, North Carolina, Ohio, South Carolina, Texas, and Virginia.

But expectations were suddenly dashed in late June 2019 when the Supreme Court ruled, in cases in Maryland and North Carolina, that partisan gerrymandering is not an activity the judiciary branch should constrain.[22] It didn't matter that in both cases defendants admitted their partisan motives. Martin O'Malley had confessed his in *USA Today*. A member of North Carolina's general assembly had admitted, "I think electing Republicans is better than electing Democrats, so I drew this map to help foster what I think is better for the country."[23] It was as if the political class had pleaded guilty and the Supreme Court refused to accept it.

On a 5–4 vote—the same margin that dooms so many political reforms—the court's conservative majority concluded that the cases presented considerations outside the legitimate reach of federal courts. The majority opinion acknowledged the dangers of the current redistricting process and suggested that reformers focus on other solutions, including ballot initiatives to create independent commissions.

The four justices on the losing end forcefully disagreed. "The partisan gerrymanders in these cases," Elena Kagan wrote in dissent, "deprived citizens of the most fundamental of their constitutional rights: the rights to participate equally in the political process, to join with others to advance political beliefs, and to choose their political representatives."[24]

Kagan went on to argue that the ruling was the first time in the court's history that a majority of justices simply washed their hands of an acknowledged constitutional violation. With three additional cases in the pipeline (Michigan, Ohio, and Wisconsin), those cases are now likely moot. The June 2019 ruling will only embolden partisans who will redraw voting maps with impunity after the 2020 census.[25]

The battle against gerrymandering has also been fought at the state level, but this can be like asking a group of foxes to fix a henhouse. In forty-two states, the redistricting process for Congress is controlled by state legislators who are not only highly partisan but who often aspire to graduate to gerrymandered congressional seats of their own. As a result, the largest advances have been made by bypassing the state legislatures and using ballot initiatives. Such referendums, which are permitted in twenty-four states, give citizens the opportunity to circumvent political insiders.

An early success came in California and could have prompted a new movie, Terminator 7: The End of Gerrymandering. In 2001, the state's congressional districts were gerrymandered so badly for political purposes that, according to FiveThirtyEight's *Gerrymandering Project*, in the next 265 elections, only one incumbent lost. That's a reelection rate of 99.6 percent. In stepped the Golden State's new governor, Arnold Schwarzenegger, who had taken office in a referendum-like recall vote. In his famous Austrian accent, the "Governator" vowed to "terminate gerrymandering." Charles Munger Jr., the son of the billionaire partner of Warren Buffett, provided financial support for this grassroots movement. Their opponents included congressional leader Nancy Pelosi.[26]

By 2010, voters passed Proposition 20. The new law created the California Citizens Redistricting Commission, required the commission to create voting districts based upon "communities of interest" and prohibited political affiliation from being considered. It was a thrilling victory for California reformers who had lost on five previous attempts to end the state's gerrymandering. In the next election in 2012, seven congressmen retired, and seven lost in the general election.

Another triumph came in Michigan, where Katie Fahey, whom I met in the months following my campaign, told me that she "made a Facebook post that accidentally started a movement to end gerrymandering."[27] Still in her twenties, Katie's enthusiasm for the cause is infectious. After her social media post, she started Voters Not Politicians, which attracted over five thousand volunteers who helped get Michigan's proposal on the ballot. Katie also enjoyed support from RepresentUs, a grassroots organization focused on federal laws that "fix our broken elections." The ensuing referendum, which passed in 2018, created the Independent Citizen Redistricting Commission now responsible for drawing Michigan's voting districts. Similar initiatives were also enacted in Colorado, Missouri, Ohio, and Utah.

When looking at the results of these anti-gerrymandering referendums, one can't help but notice their immense popularity. In Colorado, the effort took two amendments, which both passed with 70 percent of the vote. In Missouri, an amendment creating a state demographer was enacted with 62 percent of the vote. In Ohio, a constitutional amendment sailed through with 75 percent support. Only in Utah was the vote reasonably close. These statewide tallies are more evidence of Americans' support for ending gerrymandering.[28] But the best opportunity for comprehensive reform is through federal legislation.

The Solution

Item 7 of the Contract to Unite America calls for a federal law that mandates independent commissions and prohibits any consideration of party affiliation when creating congressional districts. The commissions in each state would weigh contiguity, compactness, political boundaries, and communities of interest—and then draw lines as fairly as possible.

Although the Democrats' 2019 political reform bill couldn't get a single Republican vote, its redistricting provision was well designed. Each state commission would consist of five Democrats, five Republicans, and five independents, and the recommended plan would require majority support, including at least one Democrat, one Republican, and one independent.[29]

Independent commissions are already used in Arizona, California, Hawaii, Idaho, Iowa, New Jersey, and Washington. Five other states will start in 2021: Colorado, Michigan, Missouri, Ohio, and Utah. Seven states have only one representative in the House, making redistricting irrelevant at the federal level.* In the rest, gerrymandering processes are

---

* Seven states have only one representative in the House, making redistricting irrelevant at the federal level. They are Alaska, Delaware, Montana, North Dakota, South Dakota, Vermont, and Wyoming.

controlled by partisan bodies, and it's where you can help effect change.

Gerrymandering breeds extremism and warps the connection between the American people and our representatives. Maryland's delegation should not consist almost entirely of Democrat and Republican party loyalists, and my neighbor Representative David Trone should not have a two-hundred-mile-long district. Even Martin O'Malley agrees with me. After orchestrating the state's 2011 redistricting plan, my former governor has come to see the light. He candidly concedes his admiration for Roscoe Bartlett, the moderate Republican House member whose career was ended by the Maryland Democrats' notorious "7–1" gerrymander, and is now critical of the process he once exploited.[30]

A Congress full of partisans leads to stalemate on a host of issues, including irresponsible federal deficits. "If we are to rein in our growing debt, we need to change the incentives in our political system," said Maya MacGuineas, president of the Committee for a Responsible Federal Budget. "I support independent redistricting commissions, which would be especially impactful as part of a basket of reforms to change American politics and culture." After spending more than a decade working on U.S. fiscal policy, she has concluded that our best chance for meaningful progress is through significant electoral reforms.

"Maybe as a first step toward compromise, both parties could admit that Ronald Reagan *and* Barack Obama are right. The House of Representatives was designed to be the chamber most responsive to the will of the people," David Daley wrote. "Instead, it has become impervious and insulated from it. More money flows into politics with each cycle. Mapping technology will only improve. We allow partisans of either side to continue controlling this hidden but essential function at our own peril."[31]

Republicans and Democrats who are being truthful know better than anyone how gerrymandering degrades self-government. But party insiders see themselves as being caught in a high-stakes cage match where they are fighting for survival. They instinctively punch and kick their opponent, rather than taking time to weigh the effects of their blood feud on the health of representative democracy. It's up to us to stop the carnage and fix the system. They will never do it on their own.

Contract Item 8

FAIR REPRESENTATION ACT:

Ranked-choice voting will be used in federal elections, and states with more than one member in the House of Representatives will create multimember districts of up to five members.

More Voice and Greater Choice

On November 8, 2016, voters in Maine fired a shot that wasn't heard 'round the world, but it should have been. It certainly got the attention of the duopoly. That day, Maine voters approved a ballot initiative that would require the use of ranked-choice voting (RCV) in state and congressional elections.[1] Also known as instant-runoff elections, RCV allows voters to express preferences among multiple candidates, as opposed to traditional systems where voters can express only one preference and winners can receive 40 percent or less of the vote.

Ranked-choice voting is a technical fix that sounds esoteric to those unfamiliar with the concept. But it produces immediate and profound benefits.[2] RCV encourages civility, guarantees a majority winner, opens the system to a wider pool of contenders, and increases the likelihood that pragmatic candidates will prevail.[3] For political reformers, the 2016 referendum victory was electrifying. Maine would be the first state in the union where all voters would use RCV to elect their members of Congress.[4]

The excitement was short-lived. Their fiefdoms threatened, the leaders of both major parties fought back. Maine's Republican governor, Paul LePage, incongruously called ranked-choice voting "the most horrific thing in the world."[5] Secretary of State Matt Dunlap, a Democrat, initially balked at implementing the new voting system. Dunlap lobbied legislators in both parties to repeal the law, and with LePage's support, he succeeded. In a late-night session of the Maine state legislature in October 2017, RCV was effectively repealed.[6] Elected officials in both major parties blatantly disregarded the will of their constituents.

But the tables would turn again, thanks to a provision in Maine's state constitution called a "people's veto." After several legal fights and a *second* signature drive, this one done in harsh winter weather, ranked-choice voting was again placed on the ballot for the June 2018 primary election. Once again Maine's voters approved it.[*]

History was finally made in November 2018 when RCV was used for Maine's U.S. congressional races. It had an immediate impact. In Maine's Second Congressional District, Democrat Jared Golden trailed by 2,171 votes in the first tally, but was put over the top by RCV's instant-runoff provision. Golden, who had belatedly embraced RCV, actively courted independents during the campaign.[†] Incumbent Republican representative Bruce Poliquin did not.[7]

Ranked-choice voting has been described as the "master reform." Harvard professor Larry Diamond called it "the single most promising achievable reform for making our politics more open, more civil, more democratic, and more amenable to compromise."[8] Peter Ackerman, one of the country's leading political reformers, once spent two hours passionately telling me why ranked-choice voting would be more impactful than any other single change to our electoral system. As he often does, Peter also put his money where his mouth is. He is the chairman of the Chamberlain Project and the founder of Level the Playing Field, who,

---

[*] Some 270,000 Maine residents voted on this question, compared to 210,000 who voted in both of the state's (closed) primaries combined, meaning that some 60,000 independent-minded Maine voters showed up just to weigh in on ranked-choice voting.

[†] "The ultimate irony," noted Peter Ackerman and Cara Brown McCormick in a white paper, "was that Congressman-elect Golden was part of the state legislative effort to repeal RCV."

along with John and Laura Arnold's Action Now Initiative, were the primary funders of the RCV campaign in Maine. Ackerman believes that the electorate deserves "more voice and more choice."[9]

How Does It Work?

Ranked-choice voting operates just the way you think it would. As a voter, assuming you have more than two candidates, you rank your choices. If one candidate gets over 50 percent, then the election is over. If not, the candidate with the fewest votes is eliminated, and voters who selected the last-place finisher as their first pick have their votes transferred to their second choice. In a large field, the process continues this way until one candidate gets over 50 percent. Under this method, the ultimate winner always has majority support in the final round.[10]

One reason ranked-choice voting found a receptive audience in Maine was because a number of officeholders had won three-way statewide races with only a plurality of voters' support—meaning they had been opposed by a majority of the electorate. Nine of Maine's last twelve gubernatorial elections, dating back to the 1970s, had been won with less than half the vote—and in five of those elections, the winner won with less than 40 percent of the popular vote. Governor LePage, for example, was first elected in 2010 with only 38 percent of the vote in a race where the Democrat nominee and the top independent received 19 percent and 36 percent, respectively. Republicans haven't been the only beneficiaries of this system; the two preceding governors, Democrat John Baldacci (2002) and independent Angus King (1994), won their first gubernatorial races with less than 40 percent of the vote.

Maine is not alone. In 2018, Democrats won four gubernatorial races with a plurality (Wisconsin, Nevada, Kansas, and Connecticut), and Republicans won one (Florida). While ranked-choice voting may not have changed the outcome of these races, with this voting system these five governors would have taken office with the support of a majority of voters. We wouldn't have seen a string of independents dropping out or ceasing statewide campaigns to avoid being portrayed as "spoilers," which happened in Alaska, Oregon, and Kansas. It could also open up national politics, where that argument is used as a cudgel against people even thinking of running outside the two major parties.[11]

RCV is neither unproven nor entirely new. In five Southern states, overseas voters cast ranked-choice ballots in their congressional elections.* It has also been adopted by more than twenty municipalities, including Minneapolis and Santa Fe. Two cities in Utah will implement RCV for the first time in 2019. Six more states (Alaska, Hawaii, Iowa, Kansas, Maine, and Nevada) will use RCV in the 2020 Democratic Party presidential primaries and caucuses.[12]

It's used around the world, too, in various forms, from Ireland's parliament to Papua New Guinea.[13] In Australia, ranked-choice voting is called "preferential voting," and has been employed by voters for years without any finger-pointing about "spoilers." The Aussies developed a particularly entertaining commercial extolling the system's benefits. The ad, which mocks American elections, features one woman who represents the "Shit Party" and another who represents the "Shit-Lite Party." "Together," they say, "we form the two-party system."

One of the women goes on to ask, "Do you feel like you have to vote for the lesser of two shits because if you vote for anyone else you will help the shittier party to win?"

The Academy of Motion Pictures has long used ranked-choice to

---

* The states that think ranked-choice voting is good enough for our military personnel and other citizens casting absentee ballots from abroad—but not for its residents—are Arkansas, Alabama, Louisiana, Mississippi, and South Carolina.

choose the nominees for all the major categories—and uses RCV to pick the winner of Best Picture.[14] Members of the Academy do not cast only one vote for each category but instead rank their top five in order of preference.[15] Most people understand intuitively that RCV results in nominees that more fairly reflect the preferences of the Academy.

Five Is Better Than One

Ranked-choice voting is naturally complemented by another transformative idea that sounds radical but really isn't: multimember districts. Although few Americans have thought about the logic of the current system, nothing in the Constitution requires single-member congressional districts.

Multimember districts may sound like a pipe dream, but a few states used them as recently as the 1960s for congressional elections.[16] Many states, including mine, use them for their legislatures. New congressional districts could be created with up to five members per district. Imagine combining five congressional districts in New York and using RCV to choose the representatives. Today those voters are invariably represented by five liberal Democrats. "As a conservative living in New York City," Manhattan Institute President Reihan Salam has noted, "my vote for Congress is essentially a socially approved form of venting."[17]

With RCV and multimember districts, citizens in a district that spans Queens and Brooklyn might end up with one Green Party member, three Democrats, and one Republican. Despite being from different parties, the delegation would have an incentive to work together on behalf of their shared constituents. Congress would end up with more Republicans from blue states like New York and more Democrats from red states like Texas. In Maryland, where we have eight members of

Congress, two districts would be created, each with four representatives. Residents of the western half of our state, including Montgomery County, might end up with two Democrats, one Republican and one independent in Congress. The 42 percent of taxpayers in my state who are not Democrats would, many for the first time, have true representation in Congress.

Multimember districts would also mitigate the most invidious impacts of gerrymandering. According to political scientist Lee Drutman, the United States is the world leader in gerrymandering because it is one of only a few democracies that use single-member plurality-winner districts. Only twenty-five states, those with more than five members in the House, would need any lines drawn. States like mine, with six to ten representatives, would require only one division. Only twelve states would need more than one line drawn for redistricting.[18]

David Brooks, *New York Times* columnist and influential social commentator, has praised the combination of ranked-choice voting and multimember districts as the "one reform to save America."[19]

Defending Their Turf

Would the existing duopoly resist this? Of course it would. In Maine, political insiders fought to protect the status quo even after voters made their desire for ranked-choice voting clear. This impulse is not unique to Republicans and Democrats—or even Americans. Politicians everywhere do this.

In the late 1990s, the Organization for Security and Cooperation in Europe (OSCE) evaluated potential electoral systems for Bosnia and Herzegovina, a multiethnic country formed following the collapse of the former Yugoslavia. It recommended ranked-choice voting. RCV seemed a good fit for the fledgling nation, which had three main ethnic groups, each with its own nationalist party. In the wake of a vicious sectarian civil war, Bosnia needed an electoral system that would keep the most radical leaders of each ethnic group in check and instead reward pragmatic candidates. The OSCE looked to ranked-choice voting as a way to induce pragmatic politicians to run, encourage all candidates to appeal beyond their bases, and produce winners who had received at least some support from opposing ethnic groups.

It worked this way, but only briefly. In 2000, in the first election for the three-person presidency using ranked-choice voting, the system produced a relatively moderate troika. However, before the next election in 2002, ultranationalistic party leaders colluded to eliminate RCV. Each was afraid of potentially losing power to a moderate within his ethnic group. Two years later, after the 2004 election, Bosnia ditched RCV at the local level as well. What this depressing narrative illustrates is how politicians on the ideological fringes are willing to put partisan considerations and personal ambitions ahead of their country's welfare.

I first learned about these elections from Luke Zahner, a volunteer on my campaign who had worked for the OSCE. We were having dinner with a group of campaign supporters who had bicycled with us around Maryland. As he told me the story, I marveled at the similarities between major party leaders in the United States and ultranationalists in Bosnia.

Since ranked-choice voting is such an obvious upgrade and doesn't favor one party over the other, why do politicians as different as Governor LePage and Secretary Dunlap of Maine resist it as ardently as Balkan strongmen? The answer is that our current electoral process works to their advantage.

"True reform of our political system means redistributing political power from a self-serving, two-party duopoly to the American people so that we have more choice in elections and more voice in government," says Nick Troiano, Executive Director of Unite America. "As history shows, both parties are all in favor of popular reforms up until such point where it threatens their stranglehold on power, and then they will stop at nothing to protect the status quo."[20]

This explains why party bosses from Bosnia to Maine resist even the most common-sense solutions to electoral dysfunction. In the United States, one source of their power is our winner-take-all, pluralistic voting system with single-member districts, which nearly ensures domination by two major parties. In political science, this dynamic is explained by a theory known as Duverger's Law.[21] It is named for Maurice Duverger, a French sociologist who determined in the 1950s that third parties can't compete when there is no reward for winning 10 percent, or even 20 percent, of the vote. Once two-party rule is established, the situation perpetuates itself. Politicians focus on their activist base and write off those in the middle—even in their own party. Over time the two parties and their successful politicians become increasingly radical as they each fight for control of their own base.

"The maddening things about American democracy," notes historian Theo Anderson, "are built into our legislative maps and our voting procedures; dysfunction and disenchantment are features of our electoral system, not bugs."[22]

The combination of RCV and multimember districts is the antidote.

Spoiling the Spoiler Argument

Voters are not pleased with the direction the two major parties are taking us. Sixty-eight percent of us believe that a third party is needed.[23] Yet, under the current electoral system, voters naturally move to either the Democratic or Republican candidate, largely because of the "spoiler" argument. At a county fair in Southern Maryland, one woman said to me, "I always vote for the best candidate, as long as he's not a Democrat." I understood. She's a base GOP voter. "I will never vote in a way that could cause a Democrat to win," she added.

In other words, this woman would consider voting for an independent only if she was certain it wouldn't help a Democrat. As we saw in chapter 6, this same tribal instinct caused liberals to turn against Ralph Nader, their one-time hero. But ranked-choice voting liberates such partisans from their fears. With RCV, she could have made me her first choice, listed the Republican as her second choice, free from worry that she was voting against her self-interest.

In my race, the spoiler argument was most conspicuous during the Senate confirmation hearings for U.S. Supreme Court justice Brett Kavanaugh. My team and I initially assumed that the hearings, in which U.S. senators behaved like belligerent children, would provide a boost for my campaign, which emphasized civil discourse and pragmatic solutions. Polls later showed that the opposite was true. Watching the hearings drove voters to the two poles. Those to the left of center thought they saw a group of angry white men mistreating the victim of sexual assault. Those to the right of center thought they saw the character assassination of a decent guy and highly qualified judge. There was no middle ground, which meant that few Marylanders were inclined to vote for anybody other than a Democrat or a Republican.

My friend Greg Orman had a similar experience in Kansas. In his

2014 race for the U.S. Senate, he had finished with 42.5 percent of the vote running as an independent. He had polled far enough ahead of Democratic candidate Chad Taylor that Taylor decided to drop out, making it a two-way contest between Greg and incumbent Pat Roberts. In 2018, while running again, this time for governor, Greg could never get ahead of either major party candidate and found himself portrayed by both sides as a spoiler. Despite Greg's impressive previous showing, the state's media not only robotically followed this script, it took the lead in advancing it. The Democrats began using the spoiler narrative before Greg even entered the race and repeated it relentlessly, as did the *Kansas City Star* and Kansas Public Radio. The first news story announcing his possible candidacy was dominated by voices from the two parties speculating about whether he'd help a Republican get elected. The *Star* quoted a Kansas college professor to that effect—a guy who'd been tweeting anti-Orman messages for months.[24] After positive early polling, he faded and ended up with 6.5 percent of the vote.*

Another friend, Bill Walker, encountered this dynamic in Alaska—even after winning an election. In 2014, he was elected governor as an independent after forming an alliance with the Democratic candidate, making it a two-way race between Walker and Republican incumbent Sean Parnell. But in his 2018 reelection bid, Walker got stuck in a three-way race. In October, trailing the other two candidates and not wanting to sway the result, he dropped out.

Greg's two races and Bill Walker's experience illustrate the regrettable reality for independent candidates. In a winner-take-all, pluralistic

---

* Ironically, in August 2018, an independent poll found that while Orman trailed Laura Kelly by thirteen points, in comparative head-to-head matchups with Kris Kobach, he outperformed her by double digits. The surer path to a Kobach loss would have been for the Democrat to drop out. Nonetheless, the argument that the independent candidate was the "spoiler" was never questioned.

voting system, independents who win almost always find a way to make the race a two-way contest. Under ranked-choice voting, all candidates would have an incentive to campaign vigorously to the end, the media would have reason to cover issues instead of merely the horse race, and voters would have more choice unconstrained by the highhanded spoiler argument.

Literally Joining Hands

RCV has a positive impact on elections in three ways: who becomes a candidate, how campaigns are run, and who wins elections. Let's examine each of those categories.

First, in terms of who chooses to run for political office in this country, the current system almost inevitably produces candidates from the liberal wing of the Democratic Party and the conservative wing of the Republican Party. That's who emerges when the entire system rewards extreme candidates. Moderates are discouraged from running. I can't tell you how many times friends of mine have told me that, while interested in public service, they would never run because they feel they would have to move to one political pole or the other—and neither fits them.

Peter Ackerman, in his summary of the Maine effort, wrote that voters "need to anticipate positively how (with RCV) great Americans will run, compete, and win public office without a major party affiliation. This in turn will force the two major party candidates to seek more moderate support outside their base."[25] In 2016, Michael Bloomberg said he did not run as an independent in the presidential election because his team's analysis showed that he would siphon off centrist votes from Hillary Clinton, guaranteeing Trump's election.[26] Under RCV, Bloomberg would have understood that his candidacy would not have helped Trump, and he likely would have chosen to run.

In addition, there is evidence that elections with ranked-choice voting attract more female candidates. According to RepresentWomen, founded by Cynthia Terrell, 36 percent of American cities with ranked-choice voting have women as their mayors, compared to only 23 percent of major U.S. cities.[27]

A second positive effect of RCV is that campaigns become more civil, almost as a necessity. Candidates want the second-choice votes from supporters of their opponents. They become less likely to malign rivals at every turn or spend money on negative attack ads. Issues, rather than personal onslaughts, become the focus of elections. This is not merely theoretical. FairVote, a leading national advocate of ranked-choice voting, highlights an Eagleton Poll at Rutgers University in which voters in seven cities with RCV reported "less negative campaigns."[28] The anecdotal evidence is even more heartwarming: in the 2013 race for mayor of Minneapolis, which uses RCV, in the final candidate debate, the contenders actually linked arms and sang "Kumbaya."[29] I don't expect RCV to remove all sharp elbows from campaigns, but anything that encourages unity rather than division will help heal our broken politics.*

Finally, because of the way RCV takes into account voter preferences, independents and third-party candidates would likely have a greater chance of winning, as would moderates from the two major parties. It certainly couldn't hurt. Among the 533 members of Congress (two House seats were vacant as of August 2019), only one, Justin Amash, was unaffiliated with either the Democrats or the Republicans. There were no Libertarians and no members of the Green Party. (Technically, Senators Bernie Sanders and Angus King are independents,

---

* RCV also can save tax dollars. In the 2017 mayoral election in Pueblo, Colorado, for example, sixteen candidates ran, and no one got more than 13 percent. The ensuing runoff a few weeks later cost over $100,000.

but both have become reliable Democratic votes, and Sanders has twice sought the party's nomination for president.) At a time when 46 percent of Americans identified themselves as independent, Amash was the only member of Congress who did likewise. Worse, there are fewer moderates than ever in Congress.[30]

Making It Happen

The most encompassing federal proposal, which I heartily support, is the Fair Representation Act. Introduced in 2016 by Representative Don Beyer, a Virginia Democrat, it would require states to create larger, multimember districts of up to five members and use RCV for all congressional elections.

Although ranked-choice voting is popular among voters who know about it, change of this magnitude is difficult. I have no illusions that it will be easy to gain public support for the comprehensive approach championed by FairVote and manifested in Contract Item 8. Nor does Don Beyer, whom I first met on Capitol Hill at a 2017 FairVote event, where he expressed his enthusiasm for his bill while apologizing for its "wonkiness." Ultimately, though, it is the ideal solution to the problems created by gerrymandered, winner-take-all, single-member districts.

Like all the items in the Contract to Unite America, ranked-choice voting enjoys majority support. In the Eagleton survey, 62 percent of respondents in cities with RCV favor it. Politically, it has been lauded by some of the most respected leaders within both parties. As a state senator, Barack Obama introduced legislation mandating RCV for congressional and state primary elections in Illinois. This was a reform that the future president—and his future 2008 general election opponent—agreed about.

"Instant runoff voting will lead to good government because voters will elect leaders who have the support of a majority," said John McCain in support of Alaska reformers' drive for RCV. "Elected leaders will be more likely to listen to all."[31]

While the Fair Representation Act is the ultimate goal, I understand that success will come incrementally. More public education is needed about the merits of multimember districts as well as RCV itself. The path forward begins with a state-by-state effort. Once these methods are used successfully for federal elections in a few states, beginning with Maine, we can push harder for the federal legislation that would implement the system nationally.

Making this a reality requires a national organization plus volunteers in every state. In his summary report about what it took to bring RCV about in Maine, Peter Ackerman estimates that a coordinated, fifty-state strategy will cost $200 million over ten years. Two other organizations leading the charge are FairVote, whose CEO, Rob Richie, has championed these measures for twenty-five years, and RepresentUs, led by Josh Silver, who has developed a plan to implement RCV in twenty-six states by 2024.

Each state will require a ballot initiative or a state legislative vote, and making either happen requires on-the-ground leadership. In Maine the successful effort was led by the talented partnership of Kyle Bailey, Cara McCormick, and Dick Woodbury, who together recruited thousands of volunteers and pushed the reform through two signature drives and two referendums. Kyle, whom I got to know while he managed Terry Hayes's 2018 gubernatorial campaign, told me that he is now working to expand RCV to Maine's presidential primary and general elections.

In Massachusetts, you can help Voter Choice MA, which is gaining momentum for a 2020 ballot measure. All three 2020 Massachusetts candidates for president (Republican Bill Weld and Democrats Elizabeth Warren and Seth Moulton) have indicated support for ranked-choice voting, if not for multimember districts. Even if none of them win the presidency, we need a state-by-state effort.

You could do it in your state, and hopefully you'd only have to win once, which would be half as much as what Kyle Bailey and his band of Maine volunteers had to do.

Contract Item 9

CONGRESSIONAL RULES:

Procedures in the House and Senate will be altered to reduce the power of the ideological fringes and encourage bipartisan legislation and cooperation.

A Return to Best Practices

Comprehensive immigration reform was finally about to happen—or so it seemed—in early summer 2013 when the U.S. Senate passed the Border Security, Economic Opportunity, and Immigration Modernization Act. The product of genuine compromise between Republicans and Democrats, it had been hammered out by a bipartisan working group dubbed the "Gang of Eight."*

The group of senators, four Democrats and four Republicans, had revealed the fruits of its labor three months earlier. Although their proposal gave neither side everything it wanted, it gave each side what it needed, which is what compromise means. Most important, it finally dealt with an issue that most Americans wanted (and still want) Congress to address. The proposal called for fortified law enforcement at the border and strict employment verification, while expanding temporary worker programs. It also eased pressures on so-called "dreamers" (those brought to this country as minors), added a points-based system for legal immigration, and provided a path for unauthorized immigrants to remain in the United States and eventually apply for citizenship.[1] This

---

* On the GOP side were John McCain, Lindsey Graham, Jeff Flake, and Marco Rubio, a son of immigrants. The Democratic contingent was led by Chuck Schumer and Dick Durbin along with Michael Bennet of Colorado and New Jersey's Bob Menendez, the son of Cuban refugees.

was the third time in five years that the votes on Capitol Hill appeared to be there for such a comprehensive approach. The third time would not be a charm.

The bill passed the Senate on June 27, 2013, with fourteen Republican senators voting in favor, along with every Democrat in the chamber. The final vote was 68–32.[2] It was a veto-proof majority, though a White House veto wasn't an issue: President Obama had already expressed his support. But the lopsided partisan split hinted at potential trouble in the House, then under GOP control. The big question was whether House Republicans would approve it or pass their own version of immigration reform. If so, how difficult was it going to be to reconcile a more conservative House bill with the Senate version in a House-Senate conference committee? Before the drama could build, House Speaker John Boehner issued an anticlimactic edict. He let it be known that the measure wouldn't even get a vote in his chamber. The majority party controls the legislative calendar, and Boehner said he wouldn't bring it to the floor. His explanation for this startlingly undemocratic maneuver was pure Washington-speak.

"For any legislation—including the conference report—to pass the House it's going to have to be a bill that has the support of the majority of our members," Boehner blithely told reporters.[3] By "members," Boehner was referring to the only ones who mattered to him—his fellow Republicans.

In political science, that dodge is known as the "majority of the majority rule." It's a classic example of a bad congressional habit leading to a bad result. When most Americans, and a clear majority in Congress, agree on a solution to a pressing national problem, our government should be able to make it happen. On Capitol Hill, the barrier in this case was the "Hastert rule," named after J. Dennis Hastert, a now-disgraced Illinois Republican who served as speaker from 1999 until 2007. Strictly speaking, it's not a congressional rule at all, but instead a rule of thumb, and one that epitomizes everything wrong with Washington, D.C.[4]

Its more infamous cousin is the Senate filibuster, which dates to 1805 when, almost as an afterthought, Aaron Burr invented the practice of allowing senators to hold the floor, stopping all other Senate business.*

Before running for office in 2018, I ran a company that had a few things in common with the U.S. Senate. We had about one hundred people. They were smart people, too, all with ambitions and strong opinions. Although a private sector corporation is not a democracy, we would seek compromise in order to maintain morale and momentum. On the campaign trail, I would invoke my firm and ask audiences to imagine if those in my company, or in their own organizations, showed up for work each day, half in blue uniforms and half in red, and spent their entire workday trying to discredit and demonize those wearing opposing colors. That's what the Senate has become.

In the Colonial Era town halls that molded this continent's settlers into a functioning society, citizens didn't filibuster or divide themselves into arbitrary groups—and then demand absolute fealty to that group as a parliamentary trick to thwart majority rule. They searched for consensus as the most expedient way to find solutions to pressing issues as serious as starvation.

The incentives on Capitol Hill today don't work this way. The rewards flow either to those with enough votes to ram their position

---

* Although he was vice president under Jefferson, Aaron Burr's name has been synonymous with treason for more than two centuries. Previous generations knew him as the man who tried to raise an army and carve out a portion of the United States for himself. Today, thanks to Lin-Manuel Miranda, Burr is most notorious for killing Alexander Hamilton in a duel.

down the minority's throats or to the side that simply blocks action. Either approach, cheered on by an increasingly partisan media, translates into *preventing*, rather than facilitating, sustainable problem solving.[5] As for the naysayers, former Republican Senate leader Bob Dole explained their thinking two decades ago: "If you're against something, you'd better hope there's a little gridlock."[6] In the ensuing years that candid, if slightly cynical, calculation has evolved into something more sinister. What is prized today is promoting conflict, especially if it stokes outrage within one (or both) of the two major parties' bases, which in our current system is the key to raising money and winning elections.

New Choke Points

In the imaginations of some aficionados of American politics, Senate filibusters enable a principled political outsider to stand up to corrupt machine politics. This idealistic view was reinforced by the 1939 Hollywood hit *Mr. Smith Goes to Washington.** In Frank Capra's morality play, newbie U.S. senator Jefferson Smith, portrayed by Jimmy Stewart, stands up to party bosses who are rewarding a corrupt donor by approving a needless dam to be built on land he owns at the expense of scouts whose summer camp will be flooded by the construction project. Jimmy Stewart embarks on a heroic filibuster—holding the floor and speaking all night—until the truth emerges.

---

*   *Mr. Smith Goes to Washington*, which I first saw in 1987 after being introduced to the film by my college roommate Michael Silver, has a special place in my heart. Michael's grandfather Sidney Buchman wrote the screenplay but later had his career destroyed by the McCarthy hearings. In 1951, he was forced to appear before the House Un-American Activities Committee and admit that he had been a member of the Communist Party until 1945. Buchman stood up for himself, refused to "name names," and was blacklisted by Congress.

In the real world, the filibuster is rarely employed for such noble purpose. Over the years, it has been employed for partisan or idiosyncratic reasons—or infamous ones. For more than a century, it was used by Southern senators to block racial progress, even anti-lynching legislation.[7] The record filibuster came when South Carolina's Strom Thurmond spoke on the Senate floor for twenty-four hours and eighteen minutes trying to block the landmark Civil Rights Act of 1957.[8] These days, it's used to block a wide array of legislation and presidential appointments. The senators don't even have to physically hold the floor as Thurmond did. They can merely tell the presiding officer they intend to filibuster. Until 1975, a two-thirds vote of the Senate was required to end a filibuster, a step called "cloture." That year, the rule was changed to a three-fifths majority. Those who hoped that this reform would reduce the number of filibusters were disappointed. Filibusters have become so commonplace that they are now part of the political calculus. Nothing can happen in this country without sixty senators approving.

The goal is no longer about ensuring that minorities can make themselves heard on the floor of the Senate, journalist Ezra Klein has pointed out. It's about forcing the majority to find sixty votes to pass anything. "This," Klein noted, "is not Jimmy Stewart's Washington."[9]

He's right. Use of the filibuster has grown exponentially in recent years. Until 1990, it was used 413 times in U.S. history—a rate of 2.2 times per year. Over the past dozen years, according to the group No Labels, it has been used more than six hundred times.[10] In 2003, Democrats turbocharged the process with a plan to filibuster federal appellate judges appointed by George W. Bush. The Democrats' strategy, cooked up in the offices of then–Senate majority leader Tom Daschle, was launched to scuttle the appointment of Miguel Estrada, a forty-one-year-old Honduran immigrant being groomed for a Supreme Court seat.[11] Secret memos that later came to light suggested that Senate

Democrats did not want Bush to get credit for naming the court's first Latino justice.[12] They soon applied this tactic across the board to all kinds of judges.

Predictably, this tactic came back to haunt the Democrats. After they reclaimed the Senate in 2007 and the White House the following year, they found themselves on the receiving end of Republican filibusters designed to slow-walk President Obama's judicial appointments. In 2013, Senate Democratic Leader Harry Reid responded by invoking the so-called "nuclear option," an idea that had been bandied about for a decade. Simply put, judicial nominations (except to the Supreme Court) and presidential personnel appointments requiring Senate confirmations could no longer be blocked by forty-one senators in the minority party.[13] Mitch McConnell and other Senate Republicans screamed bloody murder. Yet when they came back into power—and Democrats started filibustering President Trump's appointees—Republicans expanded the nuclear option to Supreme Court nominees. This was the parliamentary maneuver that allowed Neil Gorsuch and Brett Kavanaugh to be confirmed to the high court on party-line votes.

The filibuster is also used for other Senate business, blocking legislation—or even floor discussion—on pressing national issues. University of Miami political scientist Gregory Koger describes this development as nothing less than a "quiet revolution" that has warped the founders' intentions regarding our three branches of government.

"We have added a new veto point in American politics," he wrote. "It used to be the House, the Senate, and the President, and now it's the House, the President, the Senate majority, and the Senate minority."[14]

The Hastert rule is even worse. It arrogantly appropriates to a minority—51 percent of the majority party in one-half of the third branch of government—the power to prevent any meaningful federal legislation from passing. It does so in a chamber designed not to mimic the Senate. With its six-year terms and formal customs, the Senate was envisioned as a deliberative body that would rein in the passions of the day. The House was to have a different role. In *The Federalist Papers*, James Madison referred to the House of Representatives as the "people's House." It was to be a responsive legislative body, Madison wrote, with "an immediate dependence on, and intimate sympathy with, the people."[15]

The majority of the majority rule thwarts the founders' intentions. It breaks the connection between the will of the American people and the action on the floor of the "people's House." Hastert's press aide explained it this way: "If you pass major bills without the majority of the majority, then you tend not to be a long-term speaker." Hastert's predecessor, Newt Gingrich, explained that *his* predecessors (Tom Foley, Jim Wright, and Tip O'Neill, all Democrats) had thought this way as well. "If you can't get a majority of your members to vote yes, then a pretty prudent speaker doesn't bring it up," Gingrich said.[16] This was an admission that this practice wasn't necessarily good government. It's a good career move for the speaker himself—and all these men were career politicians.

"The House of Representatives has become a tyranny of the majority," Brookings Institution scholar Bill Galston wrote in 2018. "Speakers use their control of the Rules Committee to protect their party members from tough votes and to ensure that as many factions as possible within their party are comfortable with bills that reach the floor. Members of the minority party have virtually no say in the proceedings. As a result, the lower chamber is the place bipartisan proposals go to die."[17]

Hastert fell into the job after Gingrich was forced out and his designated successor resigned his seat over sexual infidelities. Shocked Republicans turned to Hastert, a former high school wrestling coach called "Denny" by his colleagues and invariably described as "avuncular" by the press. This was misleading. Hastert, it was later revealed, was a sexual predator in his coaching days, molesting numerous boys. He proved to be corrupt in conventional ways as well. As Hastert worked his way through the ranks of Congress, he pushed for federal highway funding that increased the value of land he secretly held by $3 million.[18] It was a con eerily similar to the one Jimmy Stewart exposed in *Mr. Smith Goes to Washington*. Hastert was later convicted of bank fraud and sent to federal prison. Although he was paroled after thirteen months, the rest of us remain stuck with a "people's House" impaired by a misbegotten rule that still bears his name.

A Better Way to Govern

In the previous chapters of this book, I have outlined reforms designed to make elections fairer and to free elected officials from the vise grip of oligarchs, special interests and absolutists in the two major political parties. This chapter, borrowing on extensive work done by No Labels and other groups and reform-minded individuals, calls for changes that could be made here and now on Capitol Hill, without waiting for better election practices.

No Labels was launched in 2011, announcing itself to the world with a book titled *Make Congress Work!* The group's operating principle has remained constant. "No Labels' crusade for bipartisanship certainly isn't popular among the conservative and progressive activists who, according to one recent study together represent less than a third of the population," says Nancy Jacobson, one of its founders. "Our organization simply wants Washington to get back to the business of working across the aisle again."[19]

The leaders of the 116th Congress themselves remember when

Washington functioned far better than it does today. Most were active on legislation that illustrates this point starkly: the North American Free Trade Agreement. Although NAFTA needs modernization and it took a beating on the 2016 campaign trail from populists on both the right (Donald Trump) and the left (Bernie Sanders), its 1993 enactment was a textbook example of bipartisanship and good governance.

Envisioned by Ronald Reagan, negotiated as a treaty by George H. W. Bush, and ultimately signed into law by Bill Clinton, NAFTA brought presidents and ex-presidents of both parties together. Gerald Ford and Jimmy Carter both made calls to wavering lawmakers to pitch the virtue of the pact.* House Speaker Thomas Foley endorsed NAFTA, but Majority Leader Dick Gephardt and Democratic Whip David Bonior were against the treaty due to the opposition of organized labor. Foley allowed them to run a rival whip operation from the U.S. Capitol, in which they rounded up votes against the treaty. Each Democratic faction buttonholed their colleagues, but they made their arguments on the merits, without name-calling or threats of retaliation.

For their part, House minority leader Bob Michel and his heir apparent, Newt Gingrich, informed Foley and the White House that to ensure NAFTA's passage, the Democratic leaders needed to deliver about one hundred votes from their side.† The final tally was 234–200, with 102 Democrats voting in favor. At the September 14, 1993, White House signing ceremony, Clinton invited Bush, Carter, and Ford to speak from the East Room podium. These were proud men who had run against each other. Jimmy Carter and Jerry Ford had by then become

---

* Some former Carter aides were surprised; they quipped among themselves that their former boss did something for Clinton he wouldn't do for himself: namely, discuss legislation with lawmakers.

† Although Gingrich was a fiery and divisive figure, Michel was the opposite. When he passed away in 2017 at ninety-seven, the headline in *Politico* read, "Ex GOP Leader Bob Michel, Face of Decency and Public Service, Dies."

close personal friends, however, and Bush, who had lost to Clinton ten months earlier, made the audience laugh when he followed Clinton to the lectern.[20] "Thank you very much," Bush began. "I thought that was a very eloquent statement by President Clinton, and now I understand why he's inside looking out, and I'm outside looking in."[21]

My point here is that politics doesn't have to be practiced the way it is now. One way to start building trust again is to reform a host of bad institutional practices on Capitol Hill—not just the filibuster and the Hastert rule—that prevent progress.

"The current rules that govern the legislative process in Washington are completely broken, which has manifested itself in a Congress that is broken," Representative Brian Fitzpatrick, a Pennsylvania Republican, said in July 2018. "The hyper-partisan, Hatfield vs. McCoy mentality in Washington D.C. must end, and I will make it my life's mission to systematically change the way business is done (and not done) in Congress."[22]

In a play on words riffing off the term "house," Washington state Democrat Derek Kilmer, added, "The House is a fixer-upper in need of renovations."[23] Kilmer and Fitzpatrick were two of the forty-eight members of the bipartisan Problem Solver Caucus, which, in late July 2018, put forward a set of reforms to the House rules it hoped to see adopted after the election. Launched in 2013 as a No Labels initiative, the caucus membership is divided evenly by party. Three-quarters of its members endorsed the package of proposed rules changes contained in a report titled "Break the Gridlock."

Among the GOP casualties in the 2018 midterms were a majority of Republican members of the Problem Solvers Caucus. At least nine lost to Democrats in November; another five did not seek reelection.*

---

* Not all the names of the twenty-four GOP Problem Solvers were made public, so their casualty rate may have been higher.

The Democrats in the caucus, who were almost all reelected, held fast to the "Break the Gridlock" agenda. Even in victory, nine of them vowed not to support a House Speaker—meaning they wouldn't vote for Nancy Pelosi—unless she agreed to reforms. Facing restive new progressive members on her left flank and a critical mass of centrist Democrats led by New Jersey representative Josh Gottheimer on her right, Pelosi agreed to negotiate.[24] This was an example of Charlie Wheelan's "fulcrum strategy" in action: in our divided politics, a relatively small number of members seeking bipartisan consensus can have an outsized impact. The upshot in this case was that Pelosi accepted a slew of changes for the 116th Congress: if a bill receives 290 co-sponsors (two-thirds of the chamber), it is now guaranteed consideration on the House floor within twenty-five days. Any amendment with more than twenty co-sponsors from each party will receive a vote on the House floor. In a return to "regular order," legislation would be subject to at least one hearing in the relevant House committee, where amendments are allowed, and any differences with Senate versions are hashed out in a House-Senate conference committee. Finally, the new rules curbed a maneuver called "the motion to vacate the chair," in which any member of the chamber can request a vote on whether to oust the speaker.

To the uninitiated, these changes may seem arcane, even trivial, especially in these fraught times we live in. But Fitzpatrick and Gottheimer told a group of No Labels supporters that they hoped to use the new rules to push through a legislative package on infrastructure improvements—the kind of issue that enjoys broad public support but can't get through a broken congressional system.

I think the tweaks in the House rules in January 2019 were a good start. Eliminating the Hastert Rule and fixing the filibuster would also help. Fulfilling Item 9 in the Contract to Unite America would entail other ambitious measures. Here are a few:

- *The speaker's gavel should be wielded by a leader of the entire House, not just the majority party.* One way to reduce hyperpartisanship would be to require a 60 percent threshold to elect the speaker. First proposed by William Galston and Elaine Kamarck in 2013, this change would almost ensure that the chamber's leader has some support from the other side of the aisle and an institutional concern for the minority party's views.[25]

- *Both chambers should end symbolic "message" bills.* With little hope of becoming law, such measures clutter the calendar and fuel mutual hostility in the chamber. In mid-summer of 2019, for example, Montana Republican senator Steve Daines called for a Senate resolution condemning socialism. I heartily support capitalism and consider socialism a proven failure. Still, Congress should not spend its time grandstanding.

- *A five-day workweek for Congress.* As recently as 1994, according to the Library of Congress, the Senate worked eighteen five-day workweeks, three times as many as in 2012, when No Labels drew attention to this issue. The House isn't much better. With more time together in Washington, lawmakers might socialize together, even across party lines as they did until the 1990s, when they were much more productive.[26]

- *Tie congressional performance to pay.* Congress has passed its spending bills on time only four times since 1952. This chaotic system virtually guarantees the misallocation of taxpayers' resources and is a big reason for our crushing national debt. Under an idea proposed in the House since 2013, members stop being paid if they missed annual deadlines for approving a federal budget or let the government shut down. "Congress is the only place in America where you get paid for showing up but not doing your work," said Representative Jim Cooper, a centrist Tennessee Democrat who sponsored the proposal again in 2019. Former representative Glenn Nye, who heads the Center for the Study of the Presidency and Congress, has also proposed that Congress is barred from raising campaign money until a federal budget is in place. I favor that as well.

+ *House must vote on all measures that receive Senate approval.* Any measure receiving sixty or more votes in the Senate should receive an automatic up-or-down vote in the House, provided it is supported by petition of a majority. Also championed by Glenn Nye, this measure would have at least guaranteed an up-or-down House vote on the 2013 immigration compromise.

+ *Streamline the presidential appointments process.* Executive branch appointees should be confirmed or rejected within ninety days of their nomination. The Senate would be required to have a floor vote within that time frame. I realize that the out-of-power party chafes at having these jobs staffed by appointees whose policies they abhor. But as President Obama told recalcitrant GOP congressional leaders in 2009, elections are supposed to have consequences. I also realize that this has been a problem for years, but the solutions proposed so far haven't fixed the problem.[27] It's time for a more forceful approach. The new president simply must be allowed to form a government.

How can ordinary Americans help? You can do so in two ways, regardless of where you live. First, encourage your member of Congress, regardless of party, to join the Problem Solvers Caucus. Second, vote for them if they do.

The bottom line here is that when a large majority of Americans and most members of Congress agree on a solution to an issue like immigration, we should be able to get something done. If the rules on Capitol Hill prevent action, well, it's time for new rules.

Contract Item 10

CREATING A CULTURE OF UNITY:

We call on our next president to form a bipartisan administration, for Congress to sign a civility pledge, for Americans to participate in national service, and for our schools to revive civics education.

Come Together Right Now

"If you had a daughter of marriageable age, would you prefer she marry a Democrat or a Republican, all other things being equal?"

In 1958, Gallup conducted a survey in which it asked people about what kind of man they wanted their daughters to marry. Leaving aside the era's casual sexism (what about sons?), the answers about political affiliation were instructive of the times. Only one-third of the Democrats surveyed said they'd prefer their daughter to marry another Democrat. Republicans were even more tolerant: only one-fourth of them indicated that it mattered at all.[1]

Today, 60 percent of Democrats and 63 percent of Republicans put partisanship ahead of romance: those are the percentages who said they'd prefer their offspring marry within their "faith," as it were.

"People in each party now share more similar views on issues and they are more alike in race and ethnicity," UCLA political scientist Lynn Vavreck has noted.[2] "Americans are increasingly surrounded by those who are like-minded—and they seem to prefer to keep it that way for the next generation."*

That's only the beginning of the mutual ill will between *D*'s and *R*'s. In the final week of the 2018 midterms, as my own race was coming to a

---

* Admittedly, those numbers are exacerbated by the ideological homogeneity of the two major parties, but it's still a striking level of clannishness.

conclusion, a SurveyMonkey poll dug further into how members of the two major parties view each other.

Look at the results:

What words would you use to describe the other party today?

Survey of U.S. adults, Oct. 30 to Nov. 2, 2018

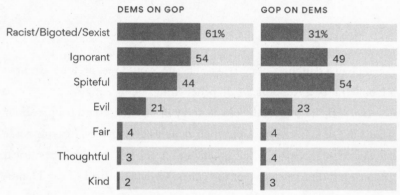

	DEMS ON GOP	GOP ON DEMS
Racist/Bigoted/Sexist	61%	31%
Ignorant	54	49
Spiteful	44	54
Evil	21	23
Fair	4	4
Thoughtful	3	4
Kind	2	3

Data provided by SurveyMonkey. Courtesy of AXIOS.

Numerous researchers have uncovered equally disturbing findings.[3] Americans have fallen into a trap set by our political leaders and deepened by a bifurcated media. In a 2017 study, Florida State University political science professor Douglas J. Ahler and independent scholar Gaurav Sood found that the average Democrat and Republican misperceives basic characteristics of the opposing party.[4] For example, typical Democrats think that more than 40 percent of Republicans earn more than $250,000 per year, and Republicans think 40 percent of Democrats are LGBTQ. They're not even close. Just 2 percent of Republicans make that level of income, and an estimated 6 percent of Democrats are LGBTQ.

Members of both parties also dramatically overestimate the percentage of the other side that holds "extreme views." Consider the actual views of Americans on immigration: a decisive majority of Republicans believe that properly controlled immigration benefits the country, while most Democrats do not believe that the United States should have open borders. However, Democrats believe that most Republicans are against all types of immigration, and Republicans think most Democrats support open borders. A nonprofit called More in Common calls this disparity "the perception gap."[5] For the immigration questions, it's 33 percentage points for each side. That's the gap for the typical Democrat or Republican.

Politicians ignite the flames of misperception with harsh, divisive rhetoric. They play up stereotypes and target their communications to their fringe supporters, who are small in number but large in political power during primaries. The media adds fuel to the fire, the study found—and as anyone who watches cable news shows critically already knows. Regular consumers of news media are nearly three times as inaccurate in their understanding of others' views when compared with those who consume news "only now and then."

Certainly, Donald Trump's rhetoric hasn't helped unite the country. Even his inaugural address sounded like a campaign stump speech.[6] And while it's a fact, not "fake news," that Russian troll farms have spread disinformation designed to exacerbate racial tensions inside the United States,[7] the sad truth is that our politicians and press have been perfectly willing to pit us against each other for partisan advantage and television ratings—without any help from the Kremlin. Liberals blame Fox News,[8] while conservatives point the finger at MSNBC,[9] CNN, and other traditional mainstream news outlets.[10]

Social media use has the same negative effect on the accuracy of how people view the other side while misleading politicians about the nature of the country.[11] Add it all up, and we have allowed an ecosystem to evolve in which politicians and media pundits are tearing our society apart. But "we, the people" have let this happen. It's time we reclaimed the levers not just of our political system, but of the national discourse itself.

The first eight chapters of this book deal with improving our elections. Chapter nine outlines the steps our current Congress could take now, without waiting for fairer election practices. This chapter, the tenth and final item in the contract, is the most ambitious of all. It's also the most inclusive and encompassing. I'm calling for changes in behavior from four groups of people: presidential candidates; every member of Congress; our nation's educators; and finally, the citizens themselves.

Specifically, this contract item calls for "unity" presidential tickets and bipartisan cabinets; civil discourse on the part of elected members of Congress; mandating civics education in our nation's public schools; and a vast expansion of national service programs until it becomes a rite of passage to give one year to our country, either in the military or as a community volunteer. These may sound like disparate measures, but they are not. They are intertwined and reinforcing. As organizations such as Renew Democracy Initiative and Service Year Alliance emphasize, creating a culture of unity begins in the heart of each American. While writing this chapter, I reached out to Unite America executive director Nick Troiano, who not only agreed with me, but who helped me formulate these ideas.

What Nick told me is that Contract Item 10 might be the most indispensable change because structural reforms won't have their intended consequence unless we figure out how to bridge the partisan divide. And that's what these four steps in Item 10 have in common— they help begin that process. "It's the most *important* because all the other things you write about may not have their desired impact until we start seeing each other and ourselves as Americans again," he told me. "And it might be the most *ambitious* because there's no legislation or ballot measures to make that happen; it's up to all of us to change the culture."

The Danger of Doing Nothing

When wealthy libertarian businessman David Koch died, the gleeful vitriol that emanated from the left was shocking, if unsurprising. Twitter was its usual cesspool, but Bill Maher reached perhaps a new low. "I'm glad he's dead," the HBO talk show host said, "and I hope the end was painful."[12]

Bette Midler managed to stoop even lower. Although her impressive volunteer efforts run the gamut from anti-littering highway cleanup efforts to helping wounded military veterans find suitable housing, Midler's idea of charity does not include political civility. When Heritage Foundation President Kay Coles James noted David Koch's passing and praised him as "a great philanthropist and friend of liberty," Midler tweeted, "With all due respect, Ms. James, fuck you."*

Such attitudes aren't merely disheartening, they are perilous. Unless we change course, things could get much worse in this country. Another poll found that nearly 60 percent of Republicans, and even more Democrats, view the opposing party as "a serious threat to the United States and its people." Asked whether they agreed that those in the other party "are downright evil," about 42 percent of Americans in each major political party answered affirmatively—significantly higher than the SurveyMonkey poll.

---

* Kay Coles James also found herself on the receiving end of a petition drive by employees at Google, after the company had asked her to join an advisory panel on artificial intelligence. She's a "white supremacist" and "vocally" anti-LGBTQ, they said. Actually, James is African American and has a gay son, with whom she is close.

These disturbing attitudes were unearthed by the academics who commissioned the survey, Louisiana State University professor Nathan P. Kalmoe and Lilliana Mason, a political scientist professor at the University of Maryland. They named this phenomenon, and their research paper, "Lethal Mass Partisanship."[13] The word "lethal" was not lightly chosen. If nearly 49 million of the 136.7 million of those who voted in 2016 equate those who voted for the other party's candidate as doing Satan's work, what are the ramifications? Kalmoe and Mason didn't shy away from exploring them. Nearly one-fifth of those surveyed agreed with the statement that those on the other side of the partisan divide "lack the traits to be considered fully human—they behave like animals."

This is the kind of rhetoric demagogues have used in totalitarian regimes to prepare the populace for genocide. So the poll respondents were asked, "Do you ever think: 'We'd be better off as a country if large numbers of the opposing party in the public today just died'?" Twenty percent of Democrats and 16 percent of Republicans answered yes. The study's authors took this sentiment to its logical conclusion:

"What if the opposing party wins the 2020 presidential election? How much do you feel violence would be justified then?" On a sliding scale of "a little" to "a lot," the survey found that 18 percent of Democrats and 14 percent of Republicans said political violence would be justified. Such aggression can't be rationalized as intemperate frustration at an anticipated loss at the ballot box. In a separate question, Kalmoe and Mason also found that *winning* elections increases the impulse for violence against the opposition.

The discovery that many Americans want their political opponents to disappear and are willing to use violence to make it happen was so startling to veteran *New York Times* political analyst Tom Edsall that he interviewed other academics to make sense of it. Among those Edsall reached out to was New York University professor Jonathan Haidt, who has extensively studied the corrosive effects of hyperpartisanship. "I am expecting that America's political dysfunction and anger will worsen," Haidt told Edsall, "and will continue to worsen even after Donald Trump leaves the White House."[14]

These concerns are not purely theoretical. The gunman in El Paso who killed twenty-two innocent people, most of them Latinos, used phrases to describe Hispanic immigrants that were indistinguishable from some of the language used by President Trump.[15] And while we can debate whether sentiments such as Bill Maher's expressed hope that his political opponents die painful deaths actually lead directly to violence, it's a matter of historic record that the gunman who wounded Representative Steve Scalise on a baseball diamond while targeting more than a dozen other Republican members of Congress on June 14, 2017, was a "Bernie Bro" motivated by partisan animus. He was an avid viewer of MSNBC, with its steady diet of anti-Republican programming.

That day, two House members of the GOP congressional baseball team needed to leave practice early. Sitting in their car, Ron DeSantis of Florida and South Carolina Representative Jeff Duncan, were approached by a man who asked if the players on the field were Republicans or Democrats.

"Republicans," they told the man, who minutes later opened fire on the GOP team. Unless we want that chilling exchange to foreshadow a general descent into political pathology, we must change direction.[16]

"President Trump is one man," proclaims Carolyn Lukensmeyer, one of the founders of National Institute for Civil Discourse.[17] "This is a democracy run by three branches of government. There are 100 people in the United States Senate and 435 in the House of Representatives. Nine justices sit on the Supreme Court. These are not just numbers. These are the men and women who have an obligation to work together to solve the issues facing our nation. We the people have an obligation to do the same."[18]

Bipartisan Administrations

The card on my desk reads, "The family of John Sidney McCain III deeply appreciates your thoughts and prayers as together we celebrate and honor the life of a loving and devoted husband, father, grandfather, loyal patriot and United States Senator."

I didn't know John McCain personally, but I admired him greatly. After his death in August 2018, I went to the Capitol Rotunda where he lay in state. During my twenty-eight years living in the Washington region, I had never seen such an intense public outpouring of emotion to the death of a senator. Waiting two hours to pay my respects, in heat so oppressive three people in the crowd fainted, seemed the least I could do for a man who sacrificed so much for our nation.

John McCain stood for honor, integrity, and service. I didn't agree with him on everything, but I believed he always put country above politics. For the next few weeks, I would talk about McCain in my stump speech. The strongest reaction from the crowd usually came when I described what McCain said was his greatest regret. A few months before he died, at the age of eighty-one and in the midst of brain cancer treatment, McCain had written that he lamented his choice of Sarah Palin as his 2008 running mate.[19] This was not a gratuitous dig at the former Alaska governor. The famous political maverick was saying that he wished he had resisted the pressures from his party and instead followed his own heart, choosing as his running mate Joe Lieberman, his good friend who happened to have once been a Democrat before becoming an Independent.

When I mentioned McCain's misgivings on the 2018 campaign trail, audiences reacted longingly at the thought of McCain-Lieberman, a presidential ticket that never was but could have been. Sometimes I would go one step further and mention that, four years before his presidential nomination, McCain himself could have been the vice presidential candidate on a 2004 unity ticket.[20] When I reminded listeners that Democratic nominee John Kerry had implored McCain to be his running mate,[21] I heard murmurs from the crowd to the effect: "I wish one of those tickets had happened; things would be so different."

Marylanders seemed hungry for leaders willing to rise above party politics to serve their country. So is the rest of the country. A 2019 poll of New Hampshire voters conducted for Unite America found that 61 percent of respondents would be supportive if "their preferred presidential candidate chose a running mate from the opposite party."[*]

Why is this concept so popular? I believe it's because most Americans yearn for a feeling of national solidarity. In these politically divided times when many citizens consider members of the opposing party evil, we have lost our sense of what it means to be an American. We long for leaders who demonstrate that the country is more important to them than their party's goals or their personal ambitions. A president who appoints a member of the opposing party as VP or as a major cabinet secretary sends a powerful signal to the nation: I am willing to risk my political career to put country above party.

Earlier in our republic, we had bipartisan administrations. John Adams, the second U.S. president, was a Federalist. His vice president,

---

[*] The precise wording of the question: "How supportive would you be if your preferred presidential candidate chose a running mate of the opposite party to create a 'Unity ticket' for president and vice-president that could unite our divided country?" Although that last phrase—"that could unite our divided country"—can be viewed as an attempt to nudge respondents toward an affirmative response, 61 percent was still impressive.

Thomas Jefferson, was from the rival Democratic-Republican Party. Back then the vice presidency was awarded to the second-place finisher in the presidential election, and Adams had beaten Jefferson by three electoral college votes in the 1796 election.* The two managed to govern together, but the framers realized that pairing electoral opponents against their wills might not be the best idea. A few years later, when the Twelfth Amendment was ratified, American voters began to elect vice presidents in separate elections. It wasn't until the Civil War era that candidates solidified the practice of a president and vice president running together on one ticket.

In his 1864 reelection bid, Republican Abraham Lincoln faced a Democratic Party nominee, George B. McClellan, who had been one of his own generals. Lincoln wanted a fusion ticket that would underscore a dual purpose. First, contrary to the stance taken by McClellan's "peace Democrats," Lincoln wanted the U.S. government to remain fully committed to the war until the Confederacy surrendered. Second, in contrast to the "Radical Republicans" on his other political flank, Lincoln hoped to send a signal to the South that he foresaw reconciliation in war's aftermath. Lincoln wanted to accomplish both those aims while also winning the 1864 election. His answer was to run under the banner of the National Unity Party, with Senator Andrew Johnson of Tennessee as his running mate. Johnson, the only Southern Democrat in the Senate who remained loyal to the Union, fit the bill perfectly.[22] "Do not talk about Republicans now; do not talk about Democrats now; do not talk about Whigs now," Johnson had said at the outbreak of the Civil War, expressing a sentiment in short supply in twenty-first

---

* Jefferson would go on to defeat Adams in the 1800 presidential election. The two, who had a contentious political relationship, became good friends in their later years. Exactly fifty years after they signed the Declaration of Independence, they both died on the same day: July 4, 1826.

century U.S. politics. "Talk about your Country and the Constitution and the Union."[23]

Blended Cabinets

Lincoln had already demonstrated the value of a bipartisan administration. He began his first term by selecting a blended cabinet. Two of its seven members, Secretary of War Edwin M. Stanton and Postmaster General Montgomery Blair, had been Democrats before the war, and Blair would be again after serving Lincoln. Among the five Republicans in his cabinet, Lincoln included three of his adversaries for the 1860 Republican presidential nomination: Secretary of State William H. Seward, Attorney General Edward Bates, and Treasury Secretary Salmon P. Chase.* National unity was more important to Lincoln than a partisan agenda, and he understood the symbolic and practical importance of including political opponents in his administration. When modern presidents have followed Lincoln's example, our country has been rewarded, sometimes when we needed it most.

On September 11, 2001, as the United States reeled from an attack on the World Trade Center and FAA officials tried to track two missing passenger jets without functioning transponders, two of the most important officials in the secure bunker under the White House known as the Presidential Emergency Operations Center were Vice President Dick Cheney and Transportation Secretary Norman Y. Mineta. The two men had known each other for years and had rarely been on the

---

* An ardent and early abolitionist, Chase was the first Republican governor of Ohio. After resigning from Lincoln's cabinet in the summer of 1864, he was appointed by the president as the sixth chief justice of the U.S. Supreme Court, in part as a way for Lincoln to keep peace with the Radical Republicans.

same side politically. As a Republican congressman from Wyoming, Cheney was one of the most conservative members of the House. Mineta, a member of the famed "Watergate babies" class of Democrats elected in 1974, was a dependable liberal voice in Congress. On that day, they were acting in concert because they were both part of George W. Bush's administration. Mineta, who left Congress in 1995, had previously served as secretary of commerce in the Clinton administration.*

The days after 9/11 was a time when America couldn't afford the indulgence of hyperpartisanship. So it came to be that the extraordinary order to thousands of pilots in the skies over this country to land their planes at the nearest airport, first issued by FAA officials, was affirmed by a Democrat—while a Republican vice president nodded his assent.[24]

Another example of a blended cabinet hit closer to home for me. In my office, on a shelf a few feet above the McCain card, I have a triptych with a photograph of myself with Hank Paulson, Ben Bernanke, and Tim Geithner. All three are intelligent, capable leaders who served our country at the highest levels. Paulson is a Republican who was appointed by George W. Bush as treasury secretary. Bernanke was a Republican who was first appointed chairman of the Federal Reserve by Bush and then reappointed by Barack Obama. Geithner, a Democrat, was the president of the Federal Reserve Bank of New York and went on to serve as Treasury secretary under President Obama.

But their powerful positions were not what I admired. It was their ability to work together, on a bipartisan basis, during the Great Recession of 2008–2009. A presidential transition is a perilous time for a democracy to experience an economic crisis, but these three public servants ignored party labels when they led our nation's resurgence from

---

* When he assumed the helm at the Department of Transportation during the Bush presidency, Mineta became only the fourth person to serve in cabinets for different political parties. Edwin Stanton had been the first.

the most wrenching financial crisis in nearly a hundred years. As the CEO of a multibillion-dollar investment firm, I had a front-row seat to the meltdown and recovery. I believe that, without the concerted efforts of this troika, the suffering of millions of Americans would have been far greater.

Of the three, I identify the most with Bernanke, who left the capital with a dim view of its partisanship. "My experience in Washington turned me off from political parties pretty completely," Bernanke concluded. "I view myself now as a moderate independent, and I think that's where I'll stay."[25]

Cross-partisan cooperation also happens at the state level. I recall fondly a campaign trip with Alaska governor Bill Walker when he told me about the cabinet he formed after being elected as an independent in 2014. We were on an Amtrak train from Washington, D.C., to New York, along with the three other independent candidates running for statewide office who had been endorsed by Unite America. Bill and I sat together while signing copies of Unite America's "Declaration of Independents,"* a set of principles by which we pledged to govern. After being elected, he explained, he chose a cabinet consisting of several Republicans, several Democrats, as well as several independents and members of smaller parties. Alaska has fifteen cabinet-level officers and another five agencies, and Walker described with a cheerful smile how someone had entered the room and seen Democrats, Republicans, Libertarians, and independents sitting there and blurted out, "What are you people?"

"We're Alaskans," Walker told them. "We're a group of Alaskans

---

* The declaration contained five sections: (a) we put the public interest ahead of any partisan or special interest, (b) we use common sense and find common ground to solve problems, (c) we stand for the timeless values of opportunity, equality, and stewardship, (d) we champion integrity, transparency, and accountability in politics, and (e) we believe in the shared responsibility of civic engagement.

doing what is best for Alaska."[26] Governor Walker believes that our leaders' loyalties should be to their country and their constituents, not to a political party. I was inspired.

Now imagine if someone entered the U.S. Capitol and asked any member of Congress the same question: "What are you?" Sadly, the instinctive answer would likely be either "I am a Republican" or "I am a Democrat." Our nation desperately needs lawmakers who think like Governor Walker and the 2008 economic trio, rather than like a group of angry NFL players in a rivalry game. The natural response of any lawmaker should be "I am an American," or "I am here to represent the people of Maryland." It should not be to announce which team they play for.

Congressional Civility

In the early years of the Obama administration, a fellow Montgomery County resident named Lanny Davis had an idea for how to encourage constructive behavior on Capitol Hill. He was a man ahead of his time. A Yale-educated lawyer who served in the Clinton administration, Davis is a loyal Democrat. He's also one of the few Americans who is friends with George W. Bush as well as Bill and Hillary Clinton, relationships that date back to their days together at Yale.* Davis, whom I don't know personally, described the name-calling and toxicity of our political discourse as "shameful" and set out to do something about it.[27]

Joining forces with Mark DeMoss, an evangelical Christian active in Republican politics, the two men launched an endeavor they called

---

* Davis attended Yale as an undergraduate, where he was a fraternity brother of Bush's; afterward, Davis stayed in New Haven to attend Yale Law School, where he became friends with Hillary Rodham and her southern boyfriend, Bill Clinton.

the Civility Project. Their initial foray into these waters was to draft a "civility pledge" consisting of three brief sentences:

+ *I will be civil in my public discourse and behavior.*

+ *I will be respectful of others whether or not I agree with them.*

+ *I will stand against incivility when I see it.*

It's a set of behavioral standards parents could reasonably ask of a second grader. Yet when they sent it to every member of the House and Senate (along with all fifty governors) what they got back was mostly crickets. Of the 585 politicians who received the pledge, almost all of them Republicans and Democrats, exactly three signed it.* Discouraged, Davis and DeMoss shuttered their Civility Project "for lack of interest" in January 2011, shortly after it began.[28]

In the interim, similar efforts have been launched. Eighteen new members of the House of Representatives signed such a pledge in 2017. Representative Mike Johnson, its author, said lawmakers should be able to "disagree without being disagreeable."[29] Other 2017 signers include Democratic Representative Ro Khanna, a progressive who served in the Commerce Department in the Obama administration and now represents a liberal Northern California congressional district, and Representative Jodey Arrington, a West Texan who worked for George W. Bush in the Austin governor's mansion and again in the White House. "You have relationships when you have that commitment to mutual respect," Arrington told *Roll Call*. "That's what civility is."[30]

The effort was sponsored by the Bipartisan Policy Center, which

---

* The three were Republican House members Sue Myrick of North Carolina, Frank Wolf of Virginia, and John McCain's old pal Joe Lieberman.

worked with key freshmen members—Representatives Jack Bergman (R-Minnesota), Val Demings (D-Florida), Nanette Barragán (D-California), and A. Donald McEachin (D-Virginia)—to hold a rally on the steps of the Capitol, recognize Johnson and the class for making civility a priority, urge the class to recommit to the pledge, and call on other members of Congress to sign it.

Some reformers I admire are skeptical of unity pledges, viewing them as symbolic gestures that are difficult to enforce. The proof, Renew Democracy Initiative executive director Uriel Epshtein believes, is whether those who sign such pledges follow up their words, with deeds: namely, are they willing to cooperate across party lines on legislation? I accept his point, but still believe such pledges are a good first step. Also, bipartisan legislating is only one facet of changing our culture. Not to sound Pollyannaish, but when it comes to changing the culture, symbolic gestures can be a good starting point. After 9/11, when Republicans and Democrats stood on the steps of the U.S. Capitol and sang "God Bless America," I think we were a better country for it.

Six years before Steve Scalise was nearly killed on the baseball diamond, another member of Congress, Arizona Democrat Gabrielle Giffords, was grievously wounded by a deranged mass shooter in Tucson. In response, Senator Mark Udall came up with a plan to have Republicans and Democrats sit together during President Obama's State of the Union Address in a show of solidarity. Udall set the tone himself, sitting next to South Carolina's Jim DeMint, one of the most conservative—and one of the most partisan—Republicans in the Senate. New York liberal Chuck Schumer sat with another conservative, Oklahoma Republican Tom Coburn.[31]

"I think if Coburn and Schumer can sit next to each other, then probably just about everybody can," Schumer said on the Sunday talk shows. Two other New Yorkers, House members Anthony Wiener and

Peter King, were seatmates, notwithstanding their history of sniping at each other. King, a Republican, described it as "stretching the outer limits of civility." Weiner quipped, "It's a nice thing. I'm going to be sitting on the Republican side, so not only will Peter King be my date, he may be my security detail also."[32] But bringing back good-natured humor was part of the point of the exercise. Meanwhile, Senator Marco Rubio, a freshman senator elected with strong Tea Party support, was paired with veteran Democratic senator Bill Nelson. And why not? They both represent the state of Florida.

In 2016, an organization called the American Congressional Exchange began flying members of Congress to districts far from home in an attempt to bridge not only partisan divides but other chasms, between East and West, the Midwest and the South, urban and rural. "Forty or fifty years ago, legislators lived in Washington," explained Jonathan Perman, the program's founder. "They got to know each other, their spouses, their children. Now the constant pressure to raise money for reelection forces them to return to their districts nearly every weekend. They don't get to know people from the other side of the aisle anymore."[33]

In the meantime, Americans aren't waiting to take their cue from Capitol Hill: many concerned folks are taking action on their own. Dozens of groups with names like With Honor, Purple America, and the National Institute for Civil Discourse have developed their own civility pledges. Others, such as Better Angels, are going about it in more creative ways, such as facilitating lunches between grassroots Democrats and Republicans and running workshops in which liberals and conservatives learn how to listen to the other side without demonizing each other.

"Our goal is nothing less than to replace the era of polarization with the era of citizenship," explained David Blankenhorn, the president and co-founder of Better Angels. "An era where we can find one another again as citizens and friends; put love of country before political faction; achieve accurate instead of exaggerated or imagined disagreement; look first for shared values and common ground; and refuse to treat our opponents as enemies."[34]

A Red, White, and Blue New Deal

At 7:00 p.m. on a cold New York night three days after Christmas 2017, a fire started in the kitchen of a first-floor complex in the Bronx. As flames raced through the mid-rise building, acrid smoke filled the hallways. Reacting quickly, twenty-seven-year-old Emmanuel Mensah hurriedly ushered a family friend and four children out of their third-floor unit downstairs to the safety of the street. He then rushed back into the inferno and was credited for rescuing four more lives.[35] He wasn't able to save himself. Overcome by smoke, he was found by NYFD first responders in a neighbor's apartment on the fourth floor, one of thirteen people who perished in the tragedy. Mensah was an immigrant from Ghana.* Although new to the country, he was deeply committed to giving back to his adopted land. He enlisted in the U.S. Army National Guard, impressing his commanding officers with the essay he wrote upon being assigned to the 16th Ordnance Battalion. Private

---

* There is nothing atypical about Emmanuel Mensah's generosity of spirit, as our family learned the previous year while spending two weeks doing public service in Yamoransa, Ghana. Jen and Sophie taught young kids English and art; my sons, Jake and Ike, taught math. I worked with "entrepreneurs," who were mainly women and who gave as much as they received. The experience—and it happened repeatedly—of being offered food in a mud hut by a Ghanaian woman for whom each day was a subsistence struggle reminded me that service is more than acts of goodwill. It's a mind-set, a lesson I relearned in West Africa.

First Class Mensah wrote about "protecting citizens and saving lives."[36]

Today, our national house is on fire. We need an infusion of his spirit. The best way I can think of doing this is universal national public service. Most of us will not pay the ultimate price, as Emmanuel Mensah did, but we can emulate his example.

A 2013 Columbia University study showed that every dollar spent on national service programs renders nearly four dollars in returns to society in terms of increased earnings, greater output, and other community-wide benefits.[37] The author of that study, Clive Belfield, notes that although almost one-quarter of the U.S. adult population does some volunteer work each year—much of it for their churches—the number devoted to organized public service programs such as Ameri-Corps, Habitat for Humanity, and Teach for America is fewer than two hundred thousand. It should be many more.

"If we had started universal national service twenty years ago," said Alan Khazei, CEO of Be the Change, "we wouldn't be in the mess we are in today."

Khazei, who was previously CEO of City Year, believes that service programs do more than strengthen communities by improving schools, parks, and housing. They do more than provide help to Americans in need. They even do more than give the volunteers experience and a sense of self-worth. National service helps bind Americans, one to the other, and to their country.

"If national service becomes a norm, then we all share a common experience," Khazei told me. "When you meet another American, you might ask 'Where did you serve?' It's a question that creates an immediate connection."

America was not founded upon a common ethnic identity. Instead, it was built on a set of ideas and values: that all men are created equal and that we each have the right to pursue life, liberty, and happiness.

The story of America is largely a story of extending those rights to new groups of Americans: enslaved people, women, the handicapped, gays, immigrants—and it's a story we should be proud of. Yet instead of celebrating that story, the dominant political culture uses our differences to divide us. Organized public service, coupled with better civic education, are paths toward returning to the principles we still share.

"Even as Americans seek to right injustices suffered by specific social groups, they need to balance their small-group identities with a more integrative identity needed to create a cohesive national democratic community," asserted Francis Fukuyama. "Liberal democracy cannot exist without a national identity that defines what citizens hold in common with one another. Given the de facto multiculturalism of contemporary democracies, that identity needs to be civic or creedal."[38]

One way to reclaim such a shared American identity is through public service programs that assemble rural and urban Americans of different races, political outlooks, and faith traditions in a common undertaking—be it planting trees, assisting the elderly, or mentoring at-risk kids. The U.S. armed forces do a pretty good job of this now, but service should be a universal experience.

"Our democracy was founded on the principle of national service," says former congressman and White House chief of staff Leon Panetta. "The patriots who stepped forward to fight our War of Independence and frame a new Constitution believed that all citizens had a duty to protect and sustain their newly established nation."

Panetta is a Democrat who was once a Republican. After leaving the GOP in the early 1970s because he believed the Nixon administration was dividing Americans for electoral advantage, Panetta wrote a book called *Bring Us Together*. Its lessons are timeless. To this day, the most obvious way to serve is to enlist in America's all-volunteer military. Maryland is home to nearly one hundred thousand active and former members of our armed forces, and during my campaign I met hundreds of them. I marveled at the country-first culture of those in uniform. None of our servicemen and women ask their commanders about political views or request to serve leaders of only one particular party. By enlisting they make a statement: they are willing to risk their lives to protect their country. Although they take pride, as they should, in belonging to the army, navy, marines, air force, or coast guard, their loyalties are to the country first. But the portion of Americans with military experience has declined from 18 percent in 1980 to only 8 percent today, so we need to provide other ways to serve.

"A service year is an extraordinary year that transforms your life and your community. It's not your typical path; it's an experience for A Better You. A Greater Us." That's the tagline for Service Year Alliance, and it captures perfectly the concept of a national service program.

"Over the past few decades, we've come to equate service with military service," says retired U.S. Army general Stanley McChrystal, the former chairman of the Joint Chiefs of Staff who heads Service Year Alliance. "In reality, service is much broader: education, healthcare, conservation. I'd like to see us expand that term 'service members' or 'people in service' as people doing the complete spectrum."[39]

In devising how to make service universal, or close to it, the first policy decision is whether it should be mandatory, which was the approach taken by Charles Rangel, the New York congressman who for years proposed national service legislation. I don't favor making it compulsory, but my hope is that over time, it would become something we all do.* Representative Seth Moulton, a Massachusetts Democrat who served

---

* There is a practical constraint on making national service compulsory. According to Alan Khazei, each year about four million Americans turn eighteen, but only a hundred thousand participate in approved service programs. It would be difficult to expand programs forty-fold while maintaining productive, efficient programs.

in the armed forces, has said in speeches that the government should work toward national service so widespread that a young adult in a job interview should expect to be asked, "Where did you do your year of service?"[40]

High schools and colleges would instill it as a core value. Employers interviewing job applicants would give preference to young people coming off their year of service. Government would administer an array of programs ranging from environmental restoration to working in schools and make participation financially feasible through job-training or educational credits along the lines of the GI Bill.

Outside the military, the largest service program is AmeriCorps, which was launched during Bill Clinton's administration. Eighty thousand Americans, of all ages and backgrounds, volunteer each year, serving for between three months and a year. They mentor kids, help veterans, maintain trails, work to alleviate poverty, and rebuild communities after natural disasters. In exchange for work, they earn an education award or a living allowance. In a true national service program, other qualifying programs could include the Peace Corps, Teach for America, Boys and Girls Clubs, and other approved nonprofits. Taking note of that history, General McChrystal laments the difficulty of making such success stories the basis for a shared national ethos.

"Arguably, not since the 1960s Peace Corps and VISTA programs has the federal government achieved major progress in the realm of national service," he has written. "Most of the action that has occurred since then has been driven by the private sector, non-governmental organizations and civic society, as with Wendy Kopp's Teach for America program for recent college graduates. All of that is well and good, but we need to bring national service up to scale and infuse it into our culture."[41]

Encouraging national service has helped unite the country in the past. In the Great Depression, President Franklin D. Roosevelt created the Civilian Conservation Corps, part of his New Deal. Men aged eighteen to twenty-four were enlisted to labor on public works programs and were paid a small wage along with food, shelter, and clothing. FDR helped 250,000 impoverished men and took historic strides for environmentalism: CCC volunteers planted three billion trees and developed hundreds of parks.

Perhaps the most famous presidential call to serve was President John F. Kennedy's plea, "Ask not what your country can do for you, ask what you can do for your country." This famous phrase is practically a mantra among the Renew Democracy Initiative Board. "The famous 'ask not' line was part of JFK's challenge to Americans and the world, not just to be good citizens, but to defend freedom," RDI board chairman Garry Kasparov told me. "It invokes grand themes of sacrifice and the responsibility of power to help others."

President George W. Bush is another believer in national service. In his first State of the Union address after the 9/11 attacks, he called on citizens to serve each other. "My call tonight is for every American to commit at least two years—4,000 hours over the rest of your lifetime—to the service of your neighbors and your nation," he said.

That's the equivalent of two working years. He understood the power of working together.

Civics Now

At his peak, Jay Leno could count on getting big laughs from his studio audience and millions of us watching at home merely by shoving a microphone in Americans' faces and asking the most rudimentary history questions imaginable.

JAY LENO: "What country did we fight in the Revolutionary War?"
DEBBIE (*from San Francisco*): "Uh, France!"
JAY LENO: "Who said, 'Give me liberty or give me death'?"
LINDA (*from Fresno*): "Bonaparte?"

And so it went, as random Americans claimed there were thirty-two stars on the U.S. flag, that Congress convened in the Pentagon, and that when Germany invaded Poland, it started "the Code War," whatever that is. Ordinary Americans couldn't name the sitting vice president (even when Leno prompted them with his first name), and never heard of the Emancipation Proclamation. It was funny, but only at first. Then it seemed sad—and ultimately alarming. This wasn't merely a Hollywood stunt. Seventy-four percent of Americans cannot name all three branches of government. That's just one of many shocking statistics in a 2017 Annenberg study that demonstrated Americans' lack of knowledge about our government.[42]

Obviously, an electorate this ignorant is easily manipulated and misled by cynical campaign consultants and opportunistic candidates of both major parties. The antidote is a massive dose of quality civics education.

Only nine states, according to CivXNow, require a full year of civics education in high school, and many existing programs are too superficial and too didactic. According to a Brookings Institution study, of the forty-two states that require at least one course related to civics education, only twenty-six include simulations of democratic processes or procedures, while only eleven states include service learning.[43] These days, these courses should also include news media literacy. The study concluded that a "lack of participatory elements of learning in state accountability frameworks highlights a void in civics education," and that "a high-quality civics education is incomplete without teaching students what civic participation looks like in practice, and how citizens can engage in their communities."

An example of an effective program is iCivics, the country's largest supplemental civics education program, which was started by former Supreme Court justice Sandra Day O'Connor and whose curriculum is used in sixty thousand schools. In the program, which is mainly for elementary and middle schoolers, students role-play being a member of Congress or a Supreme Court justice. "The practice of democracy is not passed down through the gene pool," O'Connor has said. "It must be taught and learned anew by each generation of citizens."[44]

Americans, despite their own lack of knowledge, intuitively know this. They overwhelmingly agree about the importance of learning about responsible citizenship. A nearly unanimous 97 percent of Americans say public schools should be teaching civics, including 70 percent saying it should be required, according to the PDK poll of public attitudes toward education.

Just as our country's founders considered public service vital to self-government, they deemed civics education essential to sustaining the enterprise. William H. Cabell, an early governor of Virginia, asserted in 1808 that education "constitutes one of the great pillars on which the civil liberties of a nation depend."[45]

"The Founders believed that a well-informed electorate preserves our fragile democracy and benefits American society as a whole," Harvard historian Alan Taylor has written. "More than a mere boon for individuals, education was a collective, social benefit essential for free government to endure."[46]

Columbia University professor Michael Rebell has pointed out that preparing young Americans "to be capable citizens" was one of the reasons public schools were established in the first place. In his book

Flunking Democracy: Schools, Courts and Civic Participation, Rebell shows how America's public schools have failed in this core mission of preparing young people to safeguard the nation's core democratic values.

"It's a crisis that has caught up to us in many ways," he notes, "and one we must work hard to reverse lest our representative government fall apart in future generations."[47] Rebell and Taylor are among the scholars who increasingly make a direct connection between political incivility and lousy civics education. Taylor invokes the wisdom of Declaration of Independence signer Benjamin Rush. "If the common people are ignorant and vicious," Rush observed, "a republican nation can never be long free."[48]

On this issue, I'm more prescriptive than with regards to national service. Public schools are a government function, albeit mostly a state and local one. But the federal government funds more than 8 percent of public education, and requiring civics instruction is the minimum that Washington should demand for this money.

"Mandate civics in schools (including some testing) and ensure that they not only teach the *'what'* but also the *'why,'*" Uriel Epshtein told me. "Simply teaching kids facts about their government isn't the most effective way to get them to care. If citizens don't understand *why* our democratic institutions exist, they can hardly defend them."[49]

Ted McConnell, the Executive Director of the Campaign for the Civic Mission of Schools, agrees. "When civics learning is done right, students learn constructive disagreement and respectful debate," he said to me emphatically. "It's an antidote to incivility."[50]

Imagine

When you read U.S. history, which leaders do you admire? For most of us, it's not the partisan warriors who argued doggedly and won elections but accomplished little for our country. It's the transcendent leaders who were able to forge bipartisan consensus and make progress for the American people. We respect legislators like Everett Dirksen, the collaborative Senate leader from the 1950s and 1960s whom I highlighted in this book's introduction. We revere presidents like Lincoln and FDR who had the skill and inclination to unite the nation in divided times.

If we want to revive that sense of solidarity across our country, the first step is to reset our national culture: in Washington and across all fifty states. Imagine a government where Joe Biden (D) and Mitt Romney (R) are president and vice president. Or perhaps John Kasich (R) and Amy Klobuchar (D). Or picture Donald Trump turning over a new leaf and appointing three Democrats to his cabinet. Okay, that's a stretch, but other presidents have done this kind of thing before, and we were fortunate they did. Now envision our next president working constructively with a productive Congress committed to civility. Picture millions of Americans participating in national service where they worked side by side with countrymen with opposing political views. And imagine if our children learned more about how their government functions and how to participate in our nation's civic life. Consider what America would be like if all that happened at once.

It would have made John McCain happy, and it would do us all proud.

EPILOGUE

Where We Go from Here

A few days after the 2018 election, Jen and I boarded a plane to Punta Cana. The campaign had been stressful and exhausting for both of us. We needed some R & R. As we began our descent, the flight attendant handed us a customs form for entry into the Dominican Republic. I filled out our names, address, flight information, and the purpose of our trip. The next box, which asked for occupation, rattled me. It had been a year since I had worked for my company, so writing "business executive" felt insincere. "Politician" didn't feel right either, since I had no intention of running for office again. Claiming to be an "author" never crossed my mind; I hadn't begun writing a book. After some soul searching, I wrote "Uniter."*

Bringing our country together was one reason I ran for office, and it's a goal of this book. Provoked by divisive politicians and a sectarian media, our nation is dangerously divided. We haven't experienced this level of disunity since Reconstruction. We are losing trust in each other and in our government. A few Americans have resorted to

---

* Immigration officials in the Dominican Republic apparently consider "Uniter" a valid occupation. Jen and I were granted entry to the country with no questions asked.

politically motivated violence. If we don't act, things could get worse. Recall those terrifying statistics about how 40 percent of each major party considers members of the other party "downright evil," and one in six think violence would be justified if the opposing party wins the 2020 presidential election. I don't think we are on the verge of a civil war, but that's not the America I know and love. I'm convinced we can do better.

"What concerns me most as a military man is not our external adversaries; it is our internal divisiveness," former defense secretary Jim Mattis wrote in the *Wall Street Journal*. "We are dividing into hostile tribes cheering against each other, fueled by emotion and a mutual disdain that jeopardizes our future, instead of rediscovering our common ground and finding solutions."

Today, our elected officials fuel the toxic discourse and leave us trapped in partisan gridlock on issues ranging from immigration to gun violence. Prioritizing posturing over problem solving, they are failing future generations who will be left with skyrocketing debt, deteriorating infrastructure, and exorbitant healthcare costs. If you want any of these issues to be addressed by our government, the starting point is to create incentives that attract the right leaders and encourage collaboration. Polls show that a large majority of Americans share my concern. Eighty-seven percent view dysfunctional government as our greatest national challenge—compared to 50 percent in 1990.

Democrats blame our distressing state of affairs on President Trump, while Republicans like to condemn House Democrats. But our government was divided and dysfunctional before Donald Trump ever ran for office or Nancy Pelosi became Speaker. Simply replacing Trump, whom I do not excuse for making things worse, will not solve our problems. We have a warped electoral structure that elevates the wrong kind of politicians. We, the American people, must take responsibility. Now is the time for us to dismiss discordant politicians, reject polarizing propaganda, listen to our "better angels," and become active participants in our civic life.

"We have every reason to feel mad as hell about the poor product that the U.S. Congress generates," reformer Michael Golden wrote in *Unlock Congress*. "But we do possess the power to give our representatives a better opportunity to achieve the worthwhile goals that they went to Washington to work on in the first place."

I have gotten to know Michael, an Arizona State professor, over the past two years. Clear voices like his help me remain optimistic about our country's future. But that future is not assured. We live in what academics call a "liberal democracy." It's a powerful form of government that affords us freedoms and opportunities not available in most of the world, but it's not indestructible. Liberal democracies can collapse, and they have in the past. They must be nurtured and protected and frequently require adjustments. Part of the genius of our Constitution is that it allows such upgrades.

The Founding Fathers certainly thought so. As part of a proposed preamble to an early draft of the Bill of Rights, James Madison declared, "The people have an indubitable, unalienable, and indefeasible right to reform or change their Government, whenever it be found adverse or inadequate to the purposes of its institution."

This language was borrowed from Virginia's "Declaration of Rights," a 1776 document written by Madison and George Mason. Thomas Jefferson borrowed some of its language and thinking for the Declaration of Independence. That great founding American document asserts nothing less than an "unalienable" right of the citizenry to "alter or abolish" a government no longer serving its purpose.

In our time, Katherine M. Gehl and Michael E. Porter have observed that such correctives do not happen on their own. "It is up to us as citizens to recapture our democracy—it will not be self-correcting," they wrote.

The U.S. Constitution does not mention political parties, and it makes no reference to party primaries, ballot access requirements, super PACs, the Senate filibuster, or even single-member congressional districts. This is the handiwork of Washington insiders, designed and enforced by the existing power structure for its own benefit. The Contract to Unite America—made up of the types of innovations that our nation's founders understood would periodically be required to strengthen our republic—would foster a new incentive system in which public servants would be rewarded for collaboration and getting things done for the American people.

Over the past few years, I have met dozens of reformers, some of whom have been working for decades to improve our governance. I was honored to receive the support of many of them during my campaign. While some of the proposals in my contract are original, a number are the work of others. It's a synthesis of what I consider the best ideas out there today.

By themselves, not one of my ten items is enough to restore America's promise. If we set limits on campaign funding without doing anything else, we would simply make it cheaper for the duopolists to keep control. If we implement term limits without any other changes, we would bring new representatives into a defective system. If we end gerrymandering but do not implement any of the other nine items, we only increase the competitiveness of a few congressional races. On the other hand, enacting just a few of these proposals could transform our government and civic culture.

Political elites will argue that we cannot implement these changes. "It's too hard," they will say, or "It's a pipe dream." My response is that every one of these ten contract items is supported by at least 60 percent of Americans. More electoral reform ballot initiatives were passed in 2018 than at any other time in U.S. history, with 96 percent of them approved by the electorate. Nearly every initiative enjoyed support from a majority of both Republicans and Democrats. Americans are hungry for change.

There is a proven pattern to successful political reform. Each change starts at the state level and then eventually is passed for the nation as a whole. And political innovations often happen in waves. During the Progressive Era, which spanned from the 1890s through the 1910s, Americans became socially active in a movement to correct a corrupt electoral structure and a warped economic system. Women's suffrage became the law of the land, as did direct election of senators, limits on monopolies, and ethics rules for public servants. Those changes took a couple of decades. And we shouldn't get discouraged if it takes a while to accomplish the ten contract items. We need to chip away piece by piece, and each one of us needs to do their part.

I love our country. I ran for office and lost. Losing an election is searing, but I didn't come out of it bitter. I emerged from the campaign with a deeper connection to the people of my state and our country, and I returned from my Dominican trip with a renewed desire to fight for our nation's founding principles. I did not write this book to make money, and I am not running for office. I wrote this book to provide a guide for a movement and to get more people involved. I hope you will join me in reclaiming our republic.

Become a Uniter at ContractToUnite.com.

Acknowledgments

My secret weapon in writing this book was Carl Cannon, executive editor and Washington bureau chief of RealClearPolitics. To the extent this book is anything but boring, it is due to Carl's colorful writing, his insertions of history, and his extensive knowledge of Washington politics. One day while we were working together, Carl received a response from a reader of his history-themed daily newsletter, which that day had been about the invention of ice cream cones. "Carl," she wrote, "you could make absolutely anything interesting to read." Well, I agree. I also want to thank the rest of the team at RealClearPublishing, including Naren Aryal and Kristin Perry.

Jared Alper deserves special recognition for his help with research for this book. Jared was a star of my campaign team, and I am grateful that he decided to stay on board for this project.

My wife, Jennifer, who is not just beautiful but also brilliant, provided important insights into early drafts. Jen always pushed us to answer, "What can people do to help with this issue?" Jen, please add this to the long list of things about you for which I am grateful.

I am thankful to three friends who read drafts and provided keen commentary: John Forster, Christer Johnson, and Chris Schroeder. Four other friends and family members provided invaluable editing help: Gus Bessalel, Tom Klaff, Donald Simon, and Scott Simon. I received wisdom and encouragement from my YPO forum: Brooke Coburn, Emanuel Gonzalez-Revilla, Beth Johnson, Rich Kane, Dave Pollin, Chad Sweet, and Katharine Weymouth.

I could not have written this book without the perspective I gained during my 2018 run for Senate. I want to thank my campaign team, including Steve Crim, Leah Nurick, Cynthia Findlater, Patrick Gaffney, Steven Haderlie, Latrice Jones, Eduardo Leal, Lindsey Palmer, Dane Sherrets, and my impressive group of campaign fellows. I was blessed with over two hundred volunteers, including Mike Cantwell, Harris Miller, Tom Reiter, David Silverman, and Luke Zahner. I am also appreciative of everyone who contributed financially to my campaign, particularly the dozens who hosted events or served on my finance committee. My supporters included old friends and new ones. I wish I could name you all personally here.

Over the years I grew professionally and personally because of my colleagues at Highline and Bronfman Rothschild, including my talented management team and board, to whom I am especially grateful. I have also learned a great deal from my aRIA partners and many friends, including Timor Colak, Ariel Eckstein, Michael Goodman, and Ariel Warszawski.

I'm indebted to the Unite America staff and board for their support of my campaign and their tireless work on behalf of our country. In particular, I have received assistance and wisdom in different forms from founder Charlie Wheelan, Executive Director Nick Troiano, Deputy Director Tyler Fisher, Chief of Staff Mariah Smithey, and board members Katherine Gehl, Marc Merrill, Kathryn Murdoch, Randy Peeler, Lisa Rice, and Shawn Riegsecker.

Thank you to my many other friends in the political reform movement. You inspire me. No one joins this movement for fame or fortune, or for power or prestige. You all work hard to fix our broken political system because you believe it is the right thing to do for our country. Many of you read portions of this book and contributed ideas and anecdotes. I am especially appreciative of Peter Ackerman, Daniella Ballou-Aares, Kyle Bailey, Eli Beckerman, Jeff Clements, Uriel Epshtein, Mindy Finn, John Gable, Bill Galston, Pearce Goodwin, Oliver Hall, Terry Hayes, Nancy Jacobson, Francis Johnson, Garry Kasparov, Alan Khazei, Maya MacGuineas, Ted McConnell, Evan McMullin, Cleta Mitchell, Debilyn Molineaux, David Nevins, Glenn Nye, Craig O'Dear, John Opdycke, Greg Orman, Chad Peace, Nick Penniman, John Pudner, Rob Richie, Jackie Salit, Joel Searby, Josh Silver, Paul Smith, Sterling Speirn, Rob Stein, Cynthia Terrell, Nick Tomboulides, Bill Walker, and Richard Winger.

Endnotes

Introduction

1 Maryland State Board of Elections, data as of October 22, 2018.

2 Megan Brenan, "Americans' Trust in Government to Handle Problems at New Low," Gallup, January 31, 2019.

3 "Most Important Problem," Gallup, July 2019.

4 Jill Lepore, "Long Division: Measuring the Polarization of American Politics," *The New Yorker*, December 2, 2013.

5 "PAC Dollars to Incumbents, Challengers, and Open Seat Candidates," OpenSecrets, Center for Responsive Politics, based upon data released by Federal Election Commission, June 10, 2019.

6 William A. Galston, at No Labels briefing, July 11, 2019.

7 "Annual Congressional Competitiveness Report, 2018," Ballotpedia, October 11, 2018.

8 Drew DeSilver, "Turnout in This Year's U.S. House Primaries Rose Sharply, Especially on the Democratic Side," Pew Research Center, October 3, 2018.

9 "Cost of 2018 Election to Surpass $5 Billion, CRP Projects," OpenSecrets News, October 17, 2018.

10   Peter Olsen-Phillips, Russ Choma, Sarah Bryner, and Doug Weber, "The Political One Percent in 2014: Mega Donors Fuel Rising Cost of Elections," OpenSecrets News, April 30, 2015.

11   "PAC Dollars to Incumbents, Challengers, and Open Seat Candidates," OpenSecrets, based upon data released by FEC on June 10, 2019.

12   RealClearPolitics, average of polls conducted by Reuters, Economist, Quinnipiac, Gallup and Monmouth, September 2019.

13   Katherine M. Gehl and Michael E. Porter, "Why Competition in the Politics Industry Is Failing America," Harvard Business School Publishing, September 2017.

14   Sarah Binder, "The Dysfunctional Congress," *Annual Review of Political Science*, 2015.

15   Katherine M. Gehl and Michael E. Porter, "Why Competition in the Politics Industry Is Failing America," Harvard Business School, September 2017.

16   Martin Gilens and Benjamin I. Page, "Testing Theories of American Politics: Elites, Interest Groups, and Average Americans," *American Political Science Association*, 2014.

17   Sarah A. Binder, "Polarized We Govern?" Center for Effective Public Management at Brookings, May 2014.

18   Megan Brenan, "Americans' Trust in Government to Handle Problems at New Low," Gallup, January 31, 2019.

19   Rachel L. Swarns, "Senate, in Bipartisan Act, Passes Immigration Bill; Tough Fight Is Ahead," *The New York Times*, May 26, 2006.

20   Miriam Valverde, "Did Senate Pass Immigration Bills in 2006 and 2013 and House Failed to Vote on Them?" PolitiFact, January 26, 2018.

21   Katherine M. Gehl and Michael E. Porter, "Why Competition in the Politics Industry Is Failing America," Harvard Business School, September 2017.

22 Frank H. Mackaman, "Everett Dirksen Said That?" The Dirksen Congressional Center, May 2015.

23 Charles Wheelan, *The Centrist Manifesto*, W. W. Norton & Company, New York, 2013.

24 Leadership Now Project, "Democracy Market Analysis Highlights," April 2019.

25 Ibid.

26 Sen. John McCain, address to the U.S. Senate, July 24, 2017.

Chapter 1

1 Joshua C. Huder, "The House's Competitiveness Problem," The Government Affairs Institute, Georgetown University, 2015.

2 John Opdycke, "A 50 State Open Primary Is Within Our Reach," *The Hill*, December 14, 2018.

3 League of Conservation Voters, "All Members of Congress Scores," 2018.

4 Bill Parry, "More Than a Dozen Queens Elected Officials Endorse Crowley in Primary Challenge," *Queens Courier*, May 25, 2018.

5 Jeremy Gruber, "Closed Primaries Cost Taxpayers Millions," Open Primaries press release, June 23, 2016.

6 Jonathan Rauch, "How American Politics Went Insane," *The Atlantic*, July/August 2016.

7 George E. Mowry, *The California Progressives*, University of California Press, 1951.

8 John M. Allswang, *The Initiative and Referendum in California, 1898–1998*, Stanford University Press, 2000.

9 George W. Norris, "Why I Believe in Democracy," *Annals of the American Academy of Political and Social Science*, March 1923.

10 John Jacobs, *A Rage for Justice: The Politics and Passions of Phillip Burton*, p. 40–44, University of California Press, 1995.

11 Glen Gendzel, "The People versus the Octopus: California Progressives and the Origins of Direct Democracy," Université Blaise Pascal, France, December 2013.

12 Ryan Nicol, "Poll: Majority of Florida Voters Support Primary Election Reform," *Florida Politics*, January 16, 2019.

13 John Avlon, "George Washington's Farewell Warning," *Politico*, January 10, 2017.

14 Andrew Hay, "Schultz Heckled 'Don't Elect Trump' As Eyes White House," Reuters, January 28, 2019.

15 Neal Simon and Greg Orman, "Howard Schultz, Take Your Shot," *The Wall Street Journal*, February 3, 2019.

16 *Business Wire*, November 9, 2016.

17 Brian Eason, "Open Primary Bill Advances, with Changes," *Denver Post*, May 8, 2017.

18 Author email exchange with John Opdycke, July 22, 2019.

19 Kevin Murphy, "House Bill Would Impact Missouri Primary System," *South County Times*, February 15, 2019.

20 Kurt Erickson, "Republicans Push for Closed Primaries in Missouri," *St. Louis Post-Dispatch*, May 27, 2019.

21 Alisha Shurr, "House Committee Considers Closed Primaries for Missouri Elections," *The Missouri Times*, February 20, 2019.

22 Jesse Fields, "Dr. King and the Meaning of Voting Rights," *Daily Caller*, July 14, 2017.

23 Asma Khalid, "A New Generation's Political Awakening," National Public Radio, April 21, 2018.

24 "The Generation Gap in American Politics," Pew Research Center, March 1, 2018.

25 Michael Dimock, "Defining Generations: Where Millennials End and Generation Z Begins," *Pew Research Organization*, January 17, 2019.

26 Michael Bitzer, "2017's End of the Year Analysis of NC's Voter Registration Pool," *Old North State Politics*, December 31, 2017.

Chapter 2

1 "Maryland Senate Debate," October 7, 2018, C-SPAN.

2 Brian Griffiths, "Voters Deserve Live Debates, Not Tape-Delayed Substitutes from Local TV," *Capital Gazette*, September 20, 2018.

3 Doug Donovan, "Experts Decry Single Debate Between Maryland Gov. Larry Hogan, Democrat Ben Jealous Before Election," *The Baltimore Sun*, September 10, 2018.

4 Tod Newcome, "America's Oldest Town Hall Meeting," *Governing* magazine, December 2010.

5 James Madison, "The Federalist Papers: No. 52," February 8, 1788.

6 Sean Scalmer, *On the Stump: Campaign Oratory and Democracy in the United States, Britain, and Australia*, Temple University Press, 2017.

7 Davy Crockett, *Narrative of the Life of David Crockett, of the State of Tennessee*, Carey, Hart & Co., 1834.

8 John Steele Gordon, "A Short History of Presidential Debates," *The Wall Street Journal*, October 15, 2012.

9 Andrew Glass, "1st presidential debate held, Nov. 4, 1956," *Politico*, November 4, 2014.

10 George Farah, *No Debate: How the Republican and Democratic Parties Secretly Control the Presidential Debates*, p. 170, Seven Stories Press, May 4, 2004.

11 Arianna Huffington, "Final Debate Barriers," *The Washington Times*, February 21, 2000.

12 League of Women Voters, "League Refuses to 'Help Perpetrate a Fraud'," press release, October 3, 1988.

13 David S. Broder, "Campaigns Without Shame," *The Washington Post*, September 4, 1997.

14 Jeff Cohen, "Allow Nader, Buchanan Into the Debates," *The Baltimore Sun*, September 28, 2000.

15 Newton N. Minow and Craig L. LaMay, *Inside the Presidential Debates*, p. 66, University of Chicago Press, 2008.

16 New York Times Opinions, "Fixing the Presidential Debates," *The New York Times*, September 18, 1996.

17 Connie Farrow, "Nader Sues Debate Commission," *The Washington Post*, October 17, 2000.

18 Amy Goodman, "Green Party Candidate Jill Stein's Arrest Highlights Presidential Debate Stitch-Up," *The Guardian*, October 18, 2012.

19 David Paleologos, "Paleologos on the Poll: Voters Want Third-Party Candidates on Debate Stage," *USA Today*, September 1, 2016.

20 "Green Candidates Barred From Debates and Polls in Midterms Protests Media Bias," Green Party press release, October 15, 2018.

21 Douglas Schoen, *Declaring Independence: The Beginning of the End of the Two-Party System*, p. 138, Random House, 2008.

22 Christopher Shays and Martin Meehan, "Two Former Congressmen Explain Why the Federal Elections Commission Can't Be Trusted," *The Daily Beast*, November 6, 2017.

23 Eli Beckerman, "All Politics, and All Political Transformation, Is Local," *The Fulcrum*, August 1, 2019.

Chapter 3

1 *Economist* poll, August 10–13, 2019, congressional job approval rate of 13 percent; Quinnipiac poll, July 25–28, 2019, approval rate of 14 percent; Monmouth poll, June 12–17, 2019, approval rate of 17 percent.

2 "Public Trust in Government: 1958–2019," Pew Research Center, April 11, 2019.

3 Kyle Kondik and Geoffrey Skelley, "Incumbent Reelection Rates Higher Than Average in 2016," Sabato's Crystal Ball, UVA Center for Politics, December 15, 2016.

4 "Reelection Rates Over the Years," OpenSecrets, https://www.opensecrets.org/overview/reelect.php.

5 Rasmussen Reports, March 31, 2015.

6 William T. Egar and Amber Hope Wilhelm, "Congressional Careers: Service Tenure and Patterns of Member Service: 1789–2019," Congressional Research Service, January 3, 2019.

7 "Leading with Intent: 2017 National Index of Nonprofit Board Practices," 18, Board Source, 2017.

8 Humberto Sanchez, "Fact Check: Has Chuck Schumer Ever Held a Job in the Private Sector?" Ballotpedia, June 24, 2016.

9 Interview with *National Journal*, October 23, 2010.

10 Mike DeBonis, "Will Hillary Clinton Stick with Merrick Garland if She Wins the White House?" *The Washington Post*, August 16, 2016.

11 Jenna Portnoy, "Hoyer Reflects on Partnership with Pelosi as Democrats Take Control of House," *The Washington Post*, December 31, 2018.

12 Letter from Richard Henry Lee to Edmund Randolph, Lee Family Digital Archive, October 16, 1787.

13 Jonathan Elliot, "The Debates in the Several State Conventions on the Adoption of the Federal Constitution: Volume III," Taylor & Maury, 1854.

14 Dan Balz, "Master in His House," *The Washington Post*, May 24, 1987.

15 Gerald F. Seib, "Why Watergate Lives on 40 Years After Nixon Resignation," *The Wall Street Journal*, August 4, 2014.

16 Cleta Deatherage Mitchell, "Insider Tales of an Honorable Ex-Legislator," *The Wall Street Journal*, October 11, 1990.

17 John H. Fund, "Term Limitation: An Idea Whose Time Has Come," Cato Institute, October 30, 1990.

18 Handwritten note of President Harry Truman, Truman Library, undated.

19 John H. Fund, "Term Limitation: An Idea Whose Time Has Come," Cato Institute, October 30, 1990.

20 Ibid.

21 Hendrik Hertzberg, *Politics: Observations and Arguments, 1966–2004*, 479, Penguin, 2005.

22 Ellen Goodman, "Politicians Choose Ratings Rather Than Risk," *Boston Globe*, April 8, 1990.

23 Dan Greenberg, "Term Limits: The Only Way to Clean Up Congress," The Heritage Foundation, August 10, 1994.

24 Joan Biskupic, "High Court to Hear Term-Limits Dispute," *The Washington Post*, November 28, 1994.

25 Justice John Paul Stevens, opinion of the Court, May 22, 1995.

26 Randall G. Holcombe and Robert J. Gmeiner, "Term Limits and State Budgets," *Journal of Public Finance and Public Choice*, April 2019.

27 Doug Bandow, "How to Term-Limit Congress," *National Review*, January 29, 2019.

28 John McLaughlin and Brittany Davin, "Voters Overwhelmingly Support Term Limits for Congress," McLaughlin & Associates, January 15, 2018.

29 Lindsey McPherson, "Term Limits Talks Roil House Democrats," *Roll Call*, December 12, 2018.

30 Mike Lillis, "Appetite for Democratic Term Limits Fizzling Out," *The Hill*, July 25, 2019.

31 Peter Baker, "'Nobody Should Be President for Life,' Obama Tells Africa," *The New York Times*, July 28, 2015.

32 Nick Tomboulides, Opening Remarks to Senate Judiciary Committee, June 18, 2019.

Chapter 4

1 John S. Adams, "Dark Money Group Launches Ad Attacking Rosendale," *Montana Free Press*, September 27, 2018.

2 Christina Lima and Josh Dawsey, "Clinton Lawyer, DNC Helped Bankroll Research That Led to Trump-Russia Dossier," *Politico*, October 24, 2017.

3 Reid Wilson, "Meet the Lawyer Democrats Call When It's Recount Time," *The Hill*, November 14, 2018.

4 Kenneth Vogel, "Budget Rider Would Expand Party Cash," *Politico*, December 10, 2014.

5 Wendell Potter and Nick Penniman, "Nation on the Take: How Big Money Corrupts Our Democracy and What We Can Do About It," Bloomsbury Press, February 7, 2017.

6 Maya Miller, "How the IRS Gave Up Fighting Political Dark Money Groups," *ProPublica*, April 18, 2019.

7 Garance Franke-Ruta, "Congress Put Pressure on the IRS to Investigate Conservative Tax-Exempt Groups," *The Atlantic*, May 13, 2013.

8 Sara Swann, "What the FEC Can (But Mostly Cannot) Do with Only Three Regulators on the Job," *The Fulcrum*, September 3, 2019.

9 William Gray, "Busted & Broke: Why the Federal Election Commission Doesn't Work," Issue One Blog Post, April 23, 2019.

10 Alisha Shurr, "GOP Calls for Federal Investigation Into Anonymous Anti-Hawley Mailers," *The Missouri Times*, November 2, 2018.

11 Kim Barker, "In Montana, Dark Money Helped Democrats Hold a Key Senate Seat," *ProPublica*, January 8, 2013.

12 Kevin Robillard, "Liberal Groups Spent More on Dark Money on the Midterms Than Conservative Ones Did," *Huffington Post*, January 23, 2019.

13 Matea Gold, "Koch Backed Political Network, Built to Shield Donors, Raises $400 Million in 2012 Elections," *The Washington Post*, January 5, 2014.

14 Robert Maguire, "At Least 1 in 4 Dark Money Dollars in 2012 Had Koch Links," OpenSecrets News, December 3, 2013.

15 Kenneth Vogel, "How the Kochs Launched Joni Ernst," *Politico*, November 12, 2015.

16 Louis Jacobson, "Freedom Partners Ad Accuses Rep. Bruce Braley of Giving 'Special Favors' to Insurers by Voting for Obamacare," PolitiFact, April 11, 2014.

17 Justin Jouvenal and Rachel Weiner, "PAC Funded by George Soros Pumps Nearly $1 Million Into Local Races for Prosecutor," *The Washington Post*, June 4, 2019.

Chapter 5

1 Anne M. Butler and Wendy Wolff, "*United States Senate Election, Expulsion, and Censure Cases, 1793–1990*," 263–265, Government Printing Office, June 1995.

2 Jane Hood and Lily Oberstein, "Winning with the Hand We've Got," Common Cause press release, June 6, 2018.

3 Brian Schweitzer, "Mining for Influence in Montana," *The New York Times*, June 3, 2012.

4   Irene Papanicolas, Liana R. Woskie, and Ashish K. Jha, "Health Care Spending in the United States and Other High-Income Countries," *Journal of the American Medical Association*, March 13, 2018.

5   Martin Gilens and Benjamin I. Page, "Testing Theories of American Politics: Elites, Interest Groups, and Average Citizens," American Political Science Association, September, 2014.

6   Rasmussen Reports Poll, March 31, 2015.

7   Ravi Iyer, "Money and the Financing of Campaigns," Civil Politics, 2014.

8   Stacey Selleck, "Congress Spends More Time Dialing for Dollars Than on Legislative Work," U.S. Term Limits, April 26, 2016.

9   Jasper McChesney, "How Much Time Do Congress-Members Spend Fundraising?" RepresentUS, January 30, 2018.

10   Mary Barker, "America's Hidden Primary and What You Can Do About It," Deseret News, June 26, 2014.

11   Lawrence Lessig, "We the People, and the Republic We Must Reclaim," TED Talk, April 3, 2013.

12   Scott J. Hammond, *Classics of American Political and Constitutional Thought, Volume 2: Reconstruction to the Present*, 528, Hackett Publishing Company, March 15, 2007.

13   Kim Barker and Theodoric Meyer, "The Dark Money Man: How Sean Noble Moved the Kochs' Cash into Politics and Made Millions," *ProPublica*, February 14, 2014.

14   Richard Nixon, "Statement on Signing the Federal Election Campaign Act of 1971," February 7, 1972.

15   Andy Kroll, "Follow the Dark Money," *Mother Jones*, August 2012.

16   Thomas E. Edsall, "The High Cost of Free Speech," *The New York Times*, April 8, 2014.

17   Elizabeth Kennedy, "Democratic Shame: Supreme Court Wrong on Corruption," Brennan Center for Justice, August 9, 2011.

18   David L. Hudson Jr., "Justice Thomas Making Waves in First Amendment Jurisprudence," Freedom Forum Institute, May 10, 2011.

19   David Earley and Avram Billig, "The Pro-Money Court: How the Roberts Supreme Court Dismantled Campaign Finance Law," Brennan Center for Justice, April 2, 2014.

20   Carl M. Cannon, "Debunking the Willie Horton Ad Controversy," RealClearPolitics, December 9, 2018.

21   Debra Cassens Weiss, "5–4 Citizens United Ruling a Revolution in Campaign Finance Law," *American Bar Association Journal*, January 21, 2010.

22   Mike Garibaldi, "How Far Will the Court Go to Restrict Certain Types of Speech?" *Huffington Post*, June 26, 2007.

23   Author interview with Jeff Clements, June 25, 2019.

24   Frank James, "Romney's 'Corporations are People' a Gift to Political Foes," NRP, August 11, 2011.

Chapter 6

1   Texans for Voter Choice, "Outdated, Over Regulated, and Just Plain Complicated," *Texans for Voter Choice Blog Post*, April 24, 2017.

2   Richard Winger, "A Brief History of Texas Ballot Access for Minor Parties and Independent Candidates," *Texans for Voter Choice*.

3   Alex Samuels, "It's Not Easy Being Green: Third Party Faces Long Odds to Make It onto Texas Ballot," *The Texas Tribune*, April 13, 2018.

4   Carl M. Cannon, "Kinky Witticisms," *RealClearPolitics*, November 1, 2017.

5   Patrick Svitek, "After Failing to Crash Texas' U.S. Senate Race, Independent Candidate Alleges His Petition Firm and the Cruz Campaign Derailed Him," *The Texas Tribune*, July 7, 2018.

6 Harold Meyerson, "Did the Founding Fathers Screw Up?" *The American Prospect*, September 26, 2011.

7 Oliver Hall, "Death by a Thousand Signatures: The Rise of Restrictive Ballot Access Laws and the Decline of Electoral Competition in the United States," *Seattle University Law Review*, 2005.

8 Author Interview with Richard Winger, July 21, 2009.

9 Nancy Lavin, "As U.S. Senate Candidate, Dorsey Champions the Interests of the Unaffiliated," *Frederick News Post*, November 1, 2016.

10 Jose Umana, "County Election Updates: Changes in State's Attorney Race," *Prince George's County Sentinel*, September 19, 2018.

11 Stacey Abrams, "We Cannot Resign Ourselves to Dismay and Disenfranchisement," *The New York Times*, May 15, 2019.

12 James T. Bennett, *Not Invited to the Party: How Demopublicans Have Rigged the System and Left Independents Out in the Cold*, pp. 158–160, Springer, 2009.

13 Amy Worden, "Bonusgate Tied to Campaign Against Nader," *Philadelphia Inquirer*, July 14, 2008.

14 Shankar Vedantam, "Dean and Nader Trade Barbs in Election Debate Over Election Roles," *The Washington Post*, July 10, 2014.

15 Dan Meek, "How Democrats Kicked Nader Off the Oregon Ballot," *Counter Punch Magazine*, September 28, 2004.

16 Bill Toland, "Commonwealth Court Bars Nader from Pennsylvania Ballot," *Pittsburgh Post-Gazette*, August 31, 2004.

17 Tom Infield, "Nader Letter Criticizes Pa. Courts for Knocking Him Off Ballot in 2004," *The Philadelphia Inquirer*, June 28, 2011.

18 Author interview with Oliver Hall, July 2, 2019.

19 Maria Recio, "Under Legal Attack in PA, Nader Smells Political Payback," *McClatchy Newspapers*, July 10, 2007.

20 Ibid.

21 Christopher A. Anzalone, *Supreme Court Cases on Political Representation, 1787–2001*, p. 370, M. E. Sharpe, 2002.

22 Richard Winger, "The Supreme Court and the Burial of Ballot Access: A Critical Review of Jenness v. Fortson," *Election Law Journal*, 2002.

23 Jeff Stein and Zachary Crockett, "This Is How Unhappy Americans Are with Their Choices in the Presidential Election," *Vox*, July 8, 2016.

24 Organization for Security and Co-Operation in Europe, "Existing Commitments for Democratic Elections in OSCE Participating States," OSCE Report, October 2003.

25 Jesse Rifkin, "Ballot Fairness Act Could Make It More Likely for Third-Party Congressional Candidates to Win Votes—And Maybe Elections," GovTrack Post, March 29, 2019.

26 Brian Schwartz, "Democratic Super PAC Unleashed Opposition Research Taking Aim at Starbucks Settling Lawsuits with Employees as Howard Schultz Considers 2020 Run," CNBC, February 4, 2019.

27 Bess Levin, "Howard Schultz Already Reconsidering This Whole President Thing," *Vanity Fair*, February 1, 2019.

28 Lee Drutman, William A. Galtson, Tod Lindberg, "Spoiler Alert: Why Americans' Desires for a Third Party Are Unlikely to Come True," Democracy Fund Voter Study Group, September 2018.

29 Bryan Anderson, "It's Not Just Trump. California's New Law Could Keep Other Presidential Candidates Off Its Ballot," *Sacramento Bee*, July 30, 2019.

30 Carlos Garcia, "Third-Party Candidates Suing Texas for Ballot Access," Spectrum News San Antonio, July 15, 2019.

Chapter 7

1   Christopher Ingraham, "How Maryland Democrats Pulled Off Their Aggressive Gerrymander," *The Washington Post*, March 28, 2018.

2   Dave Daley, "How Democrats Gerrymandered Their Way to Victory in Maryland," *The Atlantic*, June 25, 2017.

3   Martin O'Malley, "I Added a Democrat to Congress, But I Hope Supreme Court Ends Partisan Gerrymandering," *USA Today*, March 29, 2018.

4   Erick Trickey, "Where Did the Term 'Gerrymander' Come From?" *Smithsonian Magazine*, July 20, 2017.

5   Amanda Whiting, "Political Insiders Plotted the Most Gerrymandered District in America—and Left a Paper Trail," *Washingtonian* magazine, May 20, 2018.

6   "Cracking and Packing: Tame the Gerrymander," *The Baltimore Sun* editorial, October 3, 2017.

7   Philip J. Webster, "The Case for Jesse Colvin by a Republican," *USA Today* (Delmarva edition), September 20, 2018.

8   David Wasserman, "Final House Ratings: 75 Competitive Races, Ten Rating Changes," *The Cook Political Report*, November 5, 2018.

9   Marcy Kaptur, "My District Was Gerrymandered. The Damage Is Easy to Measure," *The Washington Post*, May 13, 2019.

10 Ibid.

11 Ronald Reagan, "Remarks at the Republican Governors Club Annual Dinner," Public Papers of the President, October 15, 1987.

12 Marshall Ingwerson, "For Californians, It May Be One Gerrymander Too Many," *The Christian Science Monitor*, October 21, 1982.

13 Michael Waldman, *The Fight to Vote*, p. 226, Simon & Schuster, 2016.

14 Bill Bishop, *The Big Sort: Why the Clustering of Like-Minded America Is Tearing Us Apart*, Houghton Mifflin, May 7, 2008.

15 David Wasserman, "Purple America Has All but Disappeared," *FiveThirtyEight*, May 8, 2017.

16 Madeline W. Lissner, "Study Reevaluates Dems' Approach," *The Harvard Crimson*, October 11, 2015.

17 Edward Blum, *The Unintended Consequences of the Voting Rights Act*, AEI Press, 2007.

18 Elizabeth Kolbert, "Drawing the Line," *The New Yorker*, June 20, 2016.

19 Campaign Legal Center, "New Bipartisan Poll Shows Support for Supreme Court to Establish Clear Rules for Gerrymandering," CLC Press Release, January 28, 2019.

20 Wallace McKelvey, "Life in Nation's Most Gerrymandered District," *Harrisburg Patriot-Ledger*, November 16, 2017.

21 Meghna Chakrabarti and Alex Schroeder, "An Unbridgeable Divide? Pennsylvania's (Ongoing) Story of Gerrymandering and Redistricting," WBUR, October 7, 2018.

22 Jess Bravin and Brent Kendall, "Supreme Court Declines to Set Limits on Political Gerrymandering," *The Wall Street Journal*, June 27, 2019.

23 Jonathan Rauch, "The Gerrymandering Ruling Was Bad, but the Alternatives Were Worse," *The Atlantic*, June 28, 2019.

24 Jake Holland and Kimberly Strawbridge Robinson, "Kagan Delivers Passionate Dissent in Redistricting Cases," *Bloomberg Law*, June 27, 2019.

25 Karen Hobert Flynn, "Supreme Court Ditches Fairness, Voter Rights and the Constitution in Gerrymandering Ruling," *USA Today*, June 27, 2019.

26 Dan Walters, "With Tables Turned, Democrats Now Oppose Gerrymandering," *The Sacramento Bee*, October 8, 2017.

27 Riley Beggin, "One Woman's Facebook Post Leads to Michigan Vote Against Gerrymandering," *Bridge Magazine*, November 7, 2018.

28 Peter Miller and Brianna Cea, "Everybody Loves Redistricting Reform," The Brennan Center for Justice, December 5, 2018.

29 Michael Li, "Five Ways H.R. 1 Would Transform Redistricting," Brennan Center blog, June 19, 2019.

30 Robert Barnes, "Democrats Did 'Duty' in Md. Redistricting. Now the Supreme Court Will Evaluate," *The Washington Post*, March 27, 2018.

31 David Daley, "The GOP Screwed Themselves: The Brilliant Gerrymander That Gave Republicans the Congress—And Created Donald Trump," *Salon*, June 6, 2016.

Chapter 8

1   Henry Grabar, "Maine Just Voted for a Better Way to Vote," *Slate*, November 9, 2016.

2   Eric Maskin, "Five Reasons Ranked-Choice Voting Will Improve American Democracy," *Boston Globe*, December 4, 2018.

3   Peter Fromuth, "Ranked-Choice Voting Is Easier Than It Sounds. Maybe It Would Cure Our Awful Politics," *USA Today*, September 6, 2018.

4   Henry Grabar, "Maine Tried a Better Way to Vote—and It's Getting Put to the Test," *Slate*, November 7, 2018.

5   Russell Berman, "Maine Voters Overrule Their Leaders," *The Atlantic*, June 15, 2018.

6   Scott Thistle, "Legislature Delays and Potentially Repeals Ranked-Choice Voting," *The Portland Press Herald*, October 24, 2017.

7   Amy Fried and Robert W. Glover, "Maine's Ranked-Choice Voting Experiment Continues," *The American Prospect*, November 20, 2018.

8   Larry Diamond, "A Victory for Democratic Reform," *The American Interest*, June 15, 2018.

9   Peter Ackerman, conversation with author, February 6, 2019.

10 Isabel Giovannetti, "Ranked-Choice Voting: How Does It Work," Common Cause Democracy Wire, August 2, 2019.

11 Alex Mealey, "It's Time to Adopt Ranked-Choice Voting Nationwide," *RealClearPolicy*, July 31, 2018.

12 Bill Theobold, "Who Knew? Ranked-Choice Voting Is Coming to the Presidential Election," *The Fulcrum*, June 12, 2019.

13 Phoenix McLaughlin, "Ranked Choice Voting in Other Countries," *Maine Meets World* blog, *Bangor Daily News*, February 16, 2016.

14 Zaid Jilani, "The Oscars Use a More Fair Voting System Than Most of America Does," *The Intercept*, March 4, 2018.

15 Nancy Lavin, "Roll Out the Red Carpet for Ranked Choice Voting at the Oscars," Fair Vote, January 11, 2019.

16 Larry F. Schaller, "Multi-Member Districts: Just a Thing of the Past?" University of Virginia Center for Politics, March 21, 2013.

17 Reihan Salam, "The Biggest Problem in American Politics," *Slate*, September 11, 2014.

18 Lee Drutman, "The Best Way to Fix Gerrymandering Is to Make It Useless," *The New York Times*, June 19, 2018.

19 David Brooks, "One Reform to Save America," *The New York Times*, May 31, 2018.

20 Author interview with Nick Troiano, August 8, 2019.

21 Chuck McCutcheon, "Speaking Politics' Term of the Week: Duverger's Law—In 10 of the Last 11 U.S. Presidential Elections, Third Parties Have Seen Their Poll Numbers Drop as the Election Draws Near. Independents Have a Better Shot at the State Level," *Christian Science Monitor*, August 9, 2016.

22 Theo Anderson, "The Two-Party System Is Facing Its Biggest Challenge in 70 Years," *In These Times*, March/April 2018.

23 Lee Drutman, William A. Galston, and Tod Lindberg, "Spoiler Alert Why Americans' Desires for a Third Party Are Unlikely to Come True," Democracy Fund Voter Study Group, September 2018.

24 Bryan Lowry and Jonathan Shorman, "Independent Greg Orman Reshuffles Race for Kansas Governor," *Kansas City Star*, December 7, 2017.

25 Peter Ackerman and Cara Brown McCormick, "Will Ranked-Choice Voting Be Adopted Nationally to Replace First-Past-the-Post Voting?" 2018.

26 Michael Bloomberg, "The Risk I Will Not Take," *Bloomberg*, March 7, 2016.

27 Cynthia Terrell, author interview, July 22, 2019.

28 Fair Vote, "Ranked Choice Voting in Practice: Candidate Civility in Ranked Choice Elections 2013 & 2014 Survey Brief," Fair Vote Study, 2013.

29 Peter Coy, "There Are Better Ways to Do Democracy," *Bloomberg Businessweek*, April 11, 2019.

30 Elaina Plott, "The 2018 Midterms Could Kill the American Moderate for Good," *The Atlantic*, November1, 2018.

31 Andy Vargas, "It's Time to Bring Ranked Choice Voting to Mass.," *CommonWealth Magazine*, July 17, 2019.

Chapter 9

1 Liz Holloran, "Gang of 8 Champion Plan, Declare 'Year of Immigration Reform'," NPR, April 13, 2013.

2 Seung Min Kim, "Senate Passes Immigration Bill," *Politico*, June 27, 2013.

3 Molly K. Hooper, "Boehner: No Immigration Vote Without 'Majority Support' of GOP Conference," *The Hill*, June 18, 2013.

4 Molly Ball, "Even the Aide Who Coined the Hastert Rule Says It Isn't Working," *The Atlantic*, July 21, 2013.

5 Jeff Jacoby, "Three Cheers for Congressional Gridlock," *Boston Globe*, November 14, 2018.

6   Sarah A. Binder, "Going Nowhere: A Gridlocked Congress," Brookings Institution, December 1, 2000.

7   Harold Meyerson, "Filibuster Nation," *The Washington Post*, August 5, 2009.

8   Tom Murse, "The 5 Longest Filibusters in History," *Thought.Co*, April 9, 2018.

9   Ezra Klein, "7 Myths About the Filibuster," *Vox*, May 27, 2015.

10 No Labels, "Five Facts: Eliminating the Filibuster," *RealClearPolicy*, February 19, 2019.

11 Marc Thiessen, "Democrats Have Only Themselves to Blame for Their Judicial Predicament," *The Washington Post*, July 6, 2018.

12 Thomas P. Carney, "'Because...He Is Latino': The Glorious History of the Democrats Filibuster Fight," *The Washington Times*, November 23, 2013.

13 Paul Kane, "Reid, Democrats Trigger 'Nuclear' Option; Eliminate Most Filibusters on Nominees," *The Washington Post*, November 21, 2013.

14 Gregory Koger, "Filibustering: A Political History of Obstruction in the House and Senate (Chicago Studies in American Politics)," University of Chicago Press, June 1, 2010.

15 James Madison, "The Federalist Papers: No. 52," *The New York Packet*, February 8, 1788.

16 Carl M. Cannon, "Down with the Hastert Rule," *RealClearPolitics*, November 30, 2014.

17 William A. Galston, "To Fix the House, Start with the Speaker," *The Wall Street Journal*, February 27, 2018.

18 Matea Gold and Anu Narayanswamy, "How Dennis Hastert Made a Fortune in Land Deals," *The Washington Post*, May 29, 2015.

19 Nancy Jacobson, "The Truth About No Labels," *RealClearPolitics*, December 7, 2018.

20 Gwen Ifill, "Clinton Recruits 3 Presidents to Promote Trade Pact," *The New York Times*, September 15, 1993.

21 Public Papers of the Presidents, September 14, 1993.

22 Ripon Advance News Service, "Bipartisan House Problem Solvers Caucus Pledges to 'Break the Gridlock' on Capitol Hill," *The Ripon Advance*, July 27, 2018.

23 *Peninsula Daily News*, "Kilmer Named Chair of New House Committee on Modernization," January 6, 2019.

24 Mike DeBonis and Robert Costa, "Pelosi and Democratic Dissidents Trade Gains in Hard Slog of Speaker's Race," *The Washington Post*, November 26, 2018.

25 William Galston and Elaine Kamarck, "Time to Change the Way We Elect Congressional Leaders," Brookings Institution, October 3, 2013.

26 "Cooper Reintroduces No Budget, No Pay Act," press release, Jim Cooper's congressional office, January 4, 2019.

27 Paul C. Light, "A Bipartisan Agenda for Presidential Appointments," *The Hill*, June 25, 2008.

Chapter 10

1 Lynn Vavreck, "A Measure of Identity: Are You Married to Your Party," *The New York Times*, January 31, 2017.

2 Ibid.

3 Ezra Klein and Alvin Chang, "Political Identity Is Fair Game for Hatred: How Republicans and Democrats Discriminate," *Vox*, December 7, 2015.

4 Douglas J. Ahler and Gaurav Sood, "The Parties in Our Heads," *The Journal of Politics*, University of Chicago Press, July 2018.

5 Sean Stevens, "The Perception Gap: How False Impressions are Pulling Americans Apart," Heredox Academy, June 28, 2019.

6 George F. Will, "A Most Dreadful Inaugural Address," *The Washington Post*, January 20, 2017.

7   Emily Stewart, "Most Russian Facebook Ads Sought to Divide Americans on Race," *Vox*, May 13, 2018.

8   Jane Mayer, "The Making of the Fox News White House," *The New Yorker*, March 11, 2019.

9   Frank Miele, "Stoking Racial Division? MSNBC Does the Dems Work," *RealClearPolitics*, August 19, 2019.

10 Becket Adams, "Daily CNN Confuse Censorious Partisanship with Journalism," *Washington Examiner*, June 3, 2019.

11 Joe Lieberman, "Social Media Is Distorting What Politicians Believe Is Real," *Time* magazine, May 16, 2018.

12 Jeanine Marie Russaw, "Bill Maher on David Koch's Death: I Hope the End Was Painful," *Newsweek*, August 24, 2019.

13 Zaid Jilani and Jeremy Adam Smith, "What's Driving Political Violence in America?" *Greater Good Magazine*, November 7, 2018.

14 Thomas B. Edsall, "No Hate Left Behind: Lethal Partisanship Is Taking Us Into Dangerous Territory," *The New York Times*, March 13, 2019.

15 Peter Baker and Michael D. Shear, "El Paso Shooting Suspect's Manifesto Echoes Trump's Language," *The New York Times*, August 4, 2019.

16 Daniella Silva, "Rep. DeSantis: Shooting Suspect Asked If 'Republicans or Democrats' on Field," NBC News, June 14, 2017.

17 Carolyn Lukensmeyer, "Incivility Will Not Fix This Crisis," *The Hill*, June 27, 2018.

18 Ibid.

19 Morgan Gstalter, "McCain Says He Regrets Picking Palin as Running Mate," *The Hill*, May 5, 2018.

20 Amy Hollyfield, "That's the Ticket," PolitiFact, February 4, 2008.

21 David M. Halbfinger, "McCain Is Said to Tell Kerry He Won't Join," *The New York Times*, June 12, 2004.

22 Joshua Zeitz, "Never Trumpers Will Want to Read This History Lesson," *Politico*, July 14, 2018.

23   Clifton R. Hall, *Andrew Johnson, Military Governor of Tennessee*, p. 28, Princeton University Press, 1916.

24   Bob Woodward and Dan Balz, "Ten Days in September," *The Washington Post*, January 22, 2002.

25   Ben. S. Bernanke, *The Courage to Act*, p. 433, W. W. Norton & Co., 2015.

26   "Only Incumbent Independent Gov. Receives Major Endorsement in Re-Election Bid," press release, the Centrist Project, October 10, 2017.

27   Carl M. Cannon, "Ten Years Later: Our Moment of Unity and Civility Was Toppled, Too," *RealClearPolitics*, September 11, 2011.

28   Ibid.

29   Alex Gangitano, "Civility Pledge Signers 'Disagree without Being Disagreeable,' in a Tumultuous Congress," *Roll Call*, December 5, 2017.

30   Ibid.

31   Devin Dwyer, "State of the Union 2011: Lawmakers Cross Aisle, Sit Together, Make History," ABC News, January 25, 2011.

32   Meredith Shiner, "Got a Date? Pols Pair Off for SOTU," *Politico*, January 22, 2011.

33   McKinley Corbley, "Congress Members from Opposing Parties Are Visiting Each Other's Districts So They Can Work Better in D.C." Good News Network, November 10, 2018.

34   Julia Mullins, "Better Angels: Bridging the Uncivil Discussion Divide," *RealClearPolitics*, June 18, 2019.

35   Elizabeth A. Harris, Ashley Southall, and Vivian Wang, "After Saving Many from Fire, Soldier Died Trying to Save One More," *The New York Times*, December 29, 2017.

36   Terrance Bell, "Face of Defense: Soldier Dies Rescuing 4 People in Burning Building," U.S. Department of Defense website, January 16, 2018.

37   "The Economic Value of National Service," Voices for National Service, September 19, 2013.

38 Francis Fukuyama, "U Pluribus Unum?" *Foreign Affairs*, March/April 2009.

39 Emily B. Hager, "Service Year: Retired Gen. Stanley McChrystal," Nation Swell, April 26, 2017.

40 Gen. Stanley McChrystal and Michael O'Hanlon, "A Focus on National Service Can Unify Our Divided Country," *The Hill*, March 2, 2019.

41 Ibid.

42 "Americans Are Poorly Informed About Basic Constitutional Provisions," Annenberg Public Policy Center, September 12, 2017.

43 Elizabeth Mann Levesque, "What Does Civics Education Look Like in America?" Brookings Education Blog, July 23, 2018.

44 Gerard Robinson, "Civil Society, Creativity, and Civic Education," American Enterprise Institute, July 27, 2016.

45 Alan Taylor, "The Virtues of an Educated Voter," *The American Scholar*, September 6, 2016.

46 Ibid.

47 Michael Rebell, "Educate to Unify: The Urgent Need for Better Civic Education in Our Dangerously Divided Nation," *New York Daily News*, October 7, 2018.

48 Ibid.

49 Email from Uriel Epshtein to author, August 24, 2019.

50 Author interview, August 7, 2019.

Bibliography

Altmire, Jason. *Dead Center: How Political Polarization Divided America and What We Can Do About It.* Mechanicsburg, Pennsylvania: Sunbury Press, 2017.

Avlon, John. *Washington's Farewell: The Founding Father's Warning to Future Generations.* New York: Simon & Schuster, 2017.

Bennett, James T. *Not Invited to the Party: How Demopublicans Have Rigged the System and Left Independents Out in the Cold.* New York: Springer, 2009.

Bernanke, Ben S. *The Courage to Act.* New York: W. W. Norton & Company, 2015.

Brill, Steven. *America's Bitter Pill: Money, Politics, Backroom Deals, and the Fight to Fix Our Broken Healthcare System.* New York: Random House, 2015.

Brill, Steven. *Tailspin. The People and Forces Behind America's Fifty-Year Fall—and Those Fighting to Reverse It.* New York: Alfred A. Knopf, 2018.

Cain, Bruce E., and Elisabeth R. Gerber. *Voting at the Political Fault Line: California's Experiment with the Blanket Primary.* Berkley, California: University of California Press, 2002.

Cannon, Lou. *Ronnie & Jesse: A Political Odyssey,* Doubleday, 1969.

Carlson, Tucker. *Ship of Fools: How a Selfish Ruling Class Is Bringing America to the Brink of Revolution*. New York: Simon & Schuster, 2018.

Clements, Jeffrey D. *Corporations Are Not People: Reclaiming Democracy from Big Money and Global Corporations*. San Francisco: Berrett-Koehler, 2014.

Conrad, Jessamyn. *What You Should Know About Politics...But Don't*. New York: Simon & Schuster, 2016.

Crockett, Davy. *The Autobiography of David Crockett*. New York: Charles Scribner's Sons, 1923.

Daley, David. *Ratf**ked: Why Your Vote Doesn't Count*. New York: Liveright Publishing, 2017.

Davis, Tom, Martin Frost, and Richard Cohen. *The Partisan Divide: Congress in Crisis*. Campbell, California: Premier, 2014.

Delaney, John K. *The Right Answer: How We Can Unify Our Divided Nation*. New York: Henry Holt, 2018.

Elliot, Jonathan. *The Debates in the Several State Conventions on the Adoption of the Federal Constitution, Volume III*. New York: Taylor & Maury, 1854.

Ellis, Joseph J. *American Dialogue: The Founders and Us*. New York: Alfred A. Knopf, 2018.

Flake, Jeff. *Conscience of a Conservative: A Rejection of Destructive Politics and a Return to Principle*. New York: Random House, 2017.

Fredrickson, Caroline. *The Democracy Fix: How to Win the Fight for Fair Rules, Fair Courts, and Fair Elections*. New York: The New Press, 2019.

Galston, William A. *Anti-Pluralism: The Populist Threat to Liberal Democracy*. New Haven, Connecticut: Yale University Press, 2018.

Gehl, Katherine M., and Michael E. Porter. *Why Competition in the Politics Industry Is Failing America*. Cambridge, Massachusetts: Harvard Business School Publishing, 2017.

Gerzon, Mark. *The Reunited States of America: How We Can Bridge the Partisan Divide*. Oakland, California: Berrett-Koehler Publishers, 2016.

Ginsburg, Tom, and Aziz Z. Huq. *How to Save a Constitutional Democracy*. Chicago: The University of Chicago Press, 2018.

Golden, Michael. *Unlock Congress: Reform the Rules, Reform the System*. Pacific Grove, California: Why Not Books, 2015.

Hall, Clifton R. *Andrew Johnson, Military Governor of Tennessee*. Princeton, New Jersey: Princeton University Press, 1916.

Hertzberg, Hendrik. *Politics: Observations and Arguments, 1966–2004*. New York: Penguin, 2005.

Jacobs, John. *A Rage for Justice: The Politics and Passions of Phillip Burton*. Berkeley, California: University of California Press, 1995.

Koger, Gregory. *Filibustering: A Political History of Obstruction in the House and Senate*. Chicago: University of Chicago Press, 2010.

Kornacki, Steve. *The Red and the Blue: The 1990s and the Birth of Political Tribalism*. New York: Ecco/HarperCollins, 2018.

Lower, Richard Coke. *A Bloc of One: The Political Career of Hiram W. Johnson*. Palo Alto, California: Stanford University Press, 1993.

Madison, James, Alexander Hamilton, and John Jay. *The Federalist Papers*. New York, 1787–1788.

Mayer, Jane. *Dark Money: The Hidden History of the Billionaires Behind the Rise of the Radical Right*. New York: First Anchor Books, 2016.

Moretti, Enrico. *The New Geography of Jobs*. New York: Houghton Mifflin Harcourt, 2012.

Mounk, Yascha. *The People vs. Democracy: Why Our Freedom Is in Danger and How to Save It.* Cambridge, Massachusetts: Harvard University Press, 2018.

Nivola, Peitro S., and David W. Brady. *Red and Blue Nation: Characteristics and Causes of America's Polarized Politics.* Washington, D.C.: Brookings Institution Press, 2006.

Orman, Greg. *A Declaration of Independents: How We Can Break the Two-Party Stranglehold and Restore the American Dream.* Austin, Texas: Greenleaf Book Group Press, 2016.

Panetta, Leon E. *Bring Us Together.* New York: J. B. Lippincott Co., 1971.

Paulson Jr., Henry M. *On the Brink: Inside the Race to Stop the Collapse of the Global Financial System.* New York: Business Plus, 2010.

Pedder, Sophie. *Revolution Francaise: Emmanuel Macron and the Quest to Reinvent a Nation.* London: Bloomsbury, 2018.

Pietila, Antero. *Not in My Neighborhood: How Bigotry Shaped a Great American City.* Chicago: Rowman & Littlefield, 2010.

Polsby, Nelson W. *How Congress Evolves: Social Bases of Institutional Change.* New York: Oxford University Press, 2004.

Potter, Wendell, and Nick Penniman. *Nation on the Take: How Big Money Corrupts Our Democracy and What We Can Do About It.* New York: Bloomsbury Press, 2016.

Rebell, Michael A. *Flunking Democracy: Schools, Courts, and Civic Participation.* Chicago: University of Chicago Press, 2018.

Sabato, Larry. *A More Perfect Constitution: 23 Proposals to Revitalize Our Constitution and Make America a Fairer Country.* New York: Walker Co., 2007.

Sasse, Ben. *Them: Why We Hate Each Other—and How to Heal.* New York: St. Martin's Press, 2018.

Scalmer, Sean. *On the Stump: Campaign Oratory and Democracy in the United States, Britain, and Australia.* Philadelphia: Temple University Press, 2017.

Schieffer, Bob, and Andrew H. Schwartz. *Finding the Truth in Today's Deluge of News*. Lanham, Maryland: Rowman & Littlefield, 2017.

Shapiro, Ira. *Broken: Can the Senate Save Itself and the Country?* Lanham, Maryland: Rowman & Littlefield, 2018.

Shapiro, Ira. *The Last Great Senate: Courage and Statesmanship in Times of Crisis*. New York: PublicAffairs, 2012.

Snyder, Timothy: *On Tyranny: Lessons from the Twentieth Century*. New York: Crown, 2017.

Sosnik, Douglas, Matthew Dowd, and Ron Fournier. *Applebee's America: How Successful Political, Business, and Religious Leaders Connect with the New American Community*. New York: Simon & Schuster, 2007.

Tribe, Laurence. *The Invisible Constitution*. New York: Oxford University Press, 2008.

Unger, Nancy C. *Fighting Bob LaFollette: The Righteous Reformer*. Chapel Hill: University of North Carolina Press, 2000.

Waldman, Michael. *The Fight to Vote*. New York: Simon & Schuster, 2016.

Wehner, Peter. *The Death of Politics: How to Heal Our Frayed Republic after Trump*. New York: HarperCollins, 2019.

Westen, Drew. *The Political Brain: The Role of Emotion in Deciding the Fate of the Nation*. New York: Public Affairs Books, 2007.

Wheelan, Charles. *The Centrist Manifesto*. New York: W. W. Norton, 2013.

Winkler, Adam. *We the Corporations: How American Businesses Won Their Civil Rights*. New York: Liveright, 2018.

Wood, Gordon S. *Friends Divided: John Adams and Thomas Jefferson*. New York: Penguin, 2017.

Index

B